RACE AND JUSTICE IN AMERICA

RACE AND JUSTICE IN AMERICA

THE CIVIL RIGHTS MOVEMENT, BLACK LIVES MATTER, AND THE WAY FORWARD

Edited by

KEVIN SCHMIESING

Race and Justice in America: The Civil Rights Movement, Black Lives Matter, and the Way Forward

© 2021 Freedom & Virtue Institute

Cover image credits:
"African American demonstrators ..." (1965):
Library of Congress, Warren K. Leffler

"Demonstrators from different cultures ..." (2020):
istockphoto, Alessandro Biascioli

Cover design by Theresa Schmiesing

ISBN: 978-1-7378879-0-4

Printed in the United States of America

Freedom & Virtue Institute
15265 New Brittany Blvd., 24W
PO Box 1320
Ft. Myers, Florida 33902
239-240-9393

CONTENTS

FOREWORD

Robert Woodson

We are living in an age when it is nearly impossible to agree what the words *race* and *justice* actually mean, let alone how to deal with the issues that surround both concepts. Into this confusion have rushed swarms of pundits, writers, journalists, "diversity" trainers, and other professionals, inundating us with their opinions about what is wrong with our country and what we are supposed to do about it. And the result is what some are calling the most polarized, unhappy time in America in living memory.

I am blessed to have more than eight decades of experience to inform my perspective on these issues. I was born in South Philadelphia in 1937, lost my father when I was still very young, and dropped out of high school at age seventeen. Almost no one in my neighborhood had a car, so my early understanding of the world was limited by where my friends and I could walk. As a result, for my entire childhood I assumed that the overwhelming majority of Americans were black, because that was what I saw around me. Needless to say, I did not feel like a "minority."

Joining the Air Force as a teenager broadened my horizons in every imaginable way. I met people from all over the country and began to travel to places I'd never even heard of. After years of not knowing what I didn't know, it finally began to dawn on me how big America—let alone the world—really was.

Today, I see a disturbingly large number of Americans whose understanding of race and justice is narrower than my understanding of the world when I only knew those few blocks in South Philly. They complain—loudly, confidently, incessantly—about issues they know almost nothing about. They do not know what they do not know.

I think a good number of those complaints—at least some of which are well-intentioned—could be addressed more productively if all of us would take the time to expand our horizons, both intellectually and experientially, to take into account the realities outside our own familiar territory and eras other than our present one. In short, to begin to understand race and justice in America today, we need to learn about places beyond America and times beyond today.

This book can help with that.

Where too many books on these issues—from both ends of the ideological spectrum—have offered only platitudes, sarcasm, and outrage, this book offers actual history and philosophy that force the reader to confront conveniently forgotten facts, to think about unfamiliar ideas, and to reconsider familiar ones.

You may not agree with everything it says, which is fine. What can we possibly learn from a book that only reaffirms what we already believe? In fact, what I hope this book will do for you and other readers is help us move beyond placing blame for America's past and get us closer to a productive debate about the best path forward.

During the civil rights movement—in which I took an active part for many years—we actually argued all the time. As much as we all shared the same goal—black liberation, broadly understood—we had passionate and sometimes seemingly insurmountable differences of opinion about how to achieve it. While elder statesmen such as Thurgood Marshall urged patience and gradual change, we younger activists bristled with frustration. While groups such as the Panthers and the Nation of Islam preached that well-armed separation and self-sufficiency were the safest way to ensure our well-being, leaders such as Dr. King thought it was vital that we work *with* whites, not *against* them.

We argued, and our arguments were nothing like the arguments I hear today. That is not to say there was never petty bickering or politics behind the scenes. Anywhere you gather human beings, you will find that. But we argued not for the purpose of bullying everyone into a single way of thinking, but to find answers and get to the heart of the matter: What *would* be the most effective way to liberate all blacks in America? What gains *should* we prioritize? And which priorities would offer the greatest improvements to the people who were suffering the most?

I left the civil rights movement when I felt its leadership was no longer trying to answer that last question in a meaningful way. After years of leading effective marches and peaceful protests, I became convinced that middle-class and wealthy blacks were reaping the majority of the movement's gains on the backs of lower income blacks. There had long been a saying that all of us were "lifting as we climbed," but it became painfully obvious to me that many of the "climbers" were stepping on the rest of us and then pulling up the ladder behind them.

That's one of those facts that doesn't fit too conveniently into the narrative around race and justice that you're most likely to hear today. Today we are told that all whites are victimizers and all blacks—however wealthy and successful—are victims. And my only response is to challenge anyone to think of a more intellectually lazy and useless analytical framework.

As much as racism is today condemned as the unforgivable sin, I have personally always found bigotry from outsiders to be far less offensive than the treason of some members of the black professional class. For example, I have never been so livid as I was when public housing residents in Washington, DC, were betrayed by members of the Congressional Black Caucus who called their proposal to own their own homes "ridiculous."[1] I have just never been able to conjure up much rage over the remarks of a few ignorant white people I will likely never meet.

Today, our so-called "debate" over issues of race and justice has gone so far off the rails that we are really just squabbling over which side gets to deploy those words as weapons in their cause du jour. And just like decades ago, the lower-income mascots for the cause get left behind, while the professional outrage-peddlers get rich.

As a grassroots leader at heart, I tend to excuse myself from intellectual discussions that are purely concerned with abstractions. What I want most is to get back to the place where we are debating the answer to that last question that still occupies my attention all these decades later: What can we do today to bring about the greatest increase in

---

[1] A fuller account of this story can be found in my book *The Triumphs of Joseph* (New York: Free Press, 1998).

the quality of life for the people in our country who are suffering the most? Rather than arguing about what race and justice mean, I would love it if we could argue about several different workable proposals to spur upward mobility, with each proponent presenting actual evidence for the efficacy of his or her preferred approach.

But to get there, we have to find a way to move past the deeply flawed understandings of race and justice in America that are so pervasive today. Our myopia on these topics is a fatal distraction from the real work before us. And my hope is, as they grapple with the information on the pages that follow, every reader will begin to do just that.

ACKNOWLEDGMENTS

The production of this book was enabled by the generosity of all of the supporters of the Freedom and Virtue Institute.

Special support was provided by the following:

Dr. Raymond Kordonowy; Congressman Francis Rooney (retired); Mr. Bob Wahlert; Mr. Gary Regoli, President/CEO of Achieva Credit Union; Mr. David H. Lucas, Chairman of the Board of The Bonita Bay Group; and Mr. and Mrs. David and Laura Thayer.

Thank you to these and all who contributed to this project.

1

THE RISE AND FALL
OF THE CIVIL RIGHTS MOVEMENT

Kevin Schmiesing

As Ismael Hernandez points out in chapter 2 of this book, slavery has been a nearly universal feature of human existence. Throughout history people have sought dominance over others, and groups of people have sought to exert control over the labor of others and thereby exploit their work for the benefit of themselves. In some cases, this exploitation has had a racial or ethnic component.

Yet the last two hundred years have witnessed powerful movements to overturn institutions of slavery. Although slavery still exists in various forms, as a legally sanctioned institution of trade and property in human beings it is virtually extinct throughout the world.[1] Indeed, for many the practice of chattel slavery such as that which prevailed in the antebellum American South is now considered the epitome of evil.

But the end of slavery in the United States did not mean that the travails of former slaves had come to an end. The racialist ideology that supported and was reinforced by slavery did not disappear with the Emancipation Proclamation. For Black Americans, a long, diffi-

---

[1] "Although the chattel form against which [anti-slavery] reformers have raged has all but disappeared, new, less visible types have arisen." Claude E. Welch Jr., "Defining Contemporary Forms of Slavery: Updating a Venerable NGO," *Human Rights Quarterly* 31, no. 1 (2009): 71, http://www.jstor.org/stable/.

cult struggle to achieve equality remained. This struggle, commonly known as the civil rights movement, is a crucial chapter in the story of America—a chapter filled with courage and cowardice, strength and frailty, moral greatness and moral failure.

It is also a story, in some ways, of decline. The unity and puissance of the movement, reaching its apex in the mid-1960s, faltered thereafter as its direction and purpose became less sharply defined. In some instances, what had been a heroic struggle to secure justice devolved into political theater and self-aggrandizement.

History admits no such thing as permanent and unmitigated victory, but by any reasonable standard the civil rights movement was a success. Recounting its story is a helpful reminder of the qualities that made it successful, and a warning against the failings that troubled its denouement. The struggle for justice for all people will never end. The history of the civil rights movement provides lessons in the ways to wage that fight—and the ways not to.

THE ABOLITION OF SLAVERY

Although many contemporary Americans think of abolitionism as a movement active in the nineteenth-century United States and composed of northerners who wished to see slavery made illegal in this country, the abolition of slavery has a long and complicated history that predates Frederick Douglass and William Lloyd Garrison by many centuries.

In the ancient world, in civilizations such as those ruled by the Egyptian, Greek, Roman, and Assyrian empires, slavery was common practice. As Christianity spread through the Roman Empire in the early centuries of the first millennium AD, the rationale for enslavement began to disintegrate. Slavery was not immediately exterminated under the sway of Christianity, but the influence of gospel teaching was instrumental in the gradual decline of the practice. The hitherto pervasive view that race, class, or sex bestowed intrinsically superior or inferior status was antithetical to Christian teaching, which was embodied in Saint Paul's insistence that "there is no longer slave or free … for all of you are one in Christ Jesus" (Gal. 3:28).[2]

---

[2] For a brief summary of the relationship of Christianity to slavery, see Jeffrey B. Russell, "Christianity and Black Slavery," *Christian Research Journal*

Christian Principles versus Slavery

The principles of the dignity and fundamental equality of all people are now taken for granted in most of the world and are perhaps the most commonly invoked ideas in western political culture. But their enthronement was not uncontested, and their application has never been complete. Their widespread acceptance was necessary, however, as a prerequisite to the dismantling of systems of human servitude.

Christian principles fueled White abolitionism as well as Black resistance to the slave system. Christian clergy made up a large part of the membership of the American Anti-Slavery Society, founded in 1833. Harriet Beecher Stowe, the daughter of the Presbyterian abolitionist minister Lyman Beecher, spurred northern abolitionism with the publication of *Uncle Tom's Cabin* in 1852.

Among slaves, Christianity offered solace for the harsh realities of slave life: "The emotional and psychological strength which enabled slaves to withstand the dehumanizing aspects of their condition came in large measure from their faith." It provided opportunities for slaves to develop their own communal structures independent of White control: "It inspired a powerful sense of community and offered leaders and spokespersons for that community." And it furnished a spiritual basis and vocabulary for resistance and the prospect of liberation: "Exodus loomed large as the fundamental narrative of the Old Testament for enslaved Christians. It convinced them that leaving slavery was not 'running away' from proper authority; it was escaping injustice."[3]

One important strand of American Black experience, originating in slavery and enduring through the succeeding decades, was religious music. M. Shawn Copeland describes its value and character:

> The spirituals are unambiguously clear that "none but the righteous shall see God" and that the wicked shall be punished, but never are these songs tainted by any scent of hatred or

36, no. 1 (2013), https://www.equip.org/article/christianity-Black-slavery/.

[3] The first two quotations are from Peter Parish, summarizing the views of influential historians: Peter J. Parish, *Slavery: History and Historians* (New York: Harper & Row, 1989), 84, 82. The third is from Jay R. Case, "Oh, Freedom: The Bible in Black Christian Movements for Liberation," *Christian History*, no. 138 (2021).

references to vengeance. The Christianity of the spirituals is a religion of reconciling, redemptive love. These songs dug the foundation for the successive waves of the struggle for freedom and civil rights and watered the stream of cultural retrieval and reappropriation. The spirituals are songs sung in hope of liberation in the context of a wilderness, but one in which God is at work, daily, hourly, to bring justice to completion.[4]

Yet religion is a large and complex reality, and Christianity can and has been used in less benign ways. Frederick Douglass castigated the "slaveholding religion" of the South; so hypocritical were publicly devout Christian slaveholders in Douglass's experience that of all slaveholders he had encountered he found "religious slaveholders the worst": "I have ever found them the meanest and basest, the most cruel and cowardly."[5] Douglass had harsh words for churchgoing people, north and south, who did not perceive the conflict between their professed beliefs and the practice of slavery. Yet he was concerned to distinguish this debased form of religion from "Christianity proper," which was "good, pure, and holy."[6] Douglass's distinctions were common for free Blacks and slaves alike, who were generally receptive to the gospel but also careful to filter out elements that did not comport with their experience. When a White, slave-owning preacher used Paul's Letter to Philemon to encourage obedience to masters, his slave listeners objected. "That is not the Gospel at all," they declared.[7]

Many professed Christians defended slavery, but their apologetics were constrained by a culture infused with Christian ideals. Most often, they adverted to the lack of explicit condemnation in the Bible or the implicit acceptance of the institution in Paul's Letter to Philemon. They asserted that Blacks' well-being required paternalistic care from slaveowners—that it was in the best interest of slaves themselves to

---

[4] M. Shawn Copeland, "*The African American Catholic Hymnal* and the African American Spiritual," in *Black Catholic Studies Reader: History and Theology*, ed. David J. Endres (Washington, DC: Catholic University of America Press, 2021), 158.

[5] Frederick Douglass, *Narrative of the Life of Frederick Douglass, an American Slave* (New York, Penguin, 1986 [1845]), 117.

[6] Douglass, *Narrative* (Appendix), 153.

[7] Case, "Oh, Freedom," 24.

be shackled. Few argued that Blacks did not deserve fair treatment or that they were a subhuman species without rights. When they did so, they departed from the mainstream Judeo-Christian mores that informed American culture and risked alienating those who might otherwise be sympathetic to southern views.

The existence of a fundamentally inhumane practice within a Christianity-dominated culture was one source of American slavery's "paradoxical" character. "The master claimed the absolute right of an owner over his property," historian Peter J. Parish observes, "but he was also restrained by the conventional morality of his time, his own standards of decency, the precepts of his religious faith, and the pressure of the White community."[8] In sum, slavery's friends and foes alike were compelled to debate within the idiom of a Christian worldview that held individual dignity sacred. Whichever side could most compellingly identify its position with that worldview would gain the upper hand.[9]

We know how that story ended—which is not to say that the fight was not bitter, chaotic, and ultimately bloody. Through the crucible of the Civil War was forged emancipation, first of southern slaves and then of all enslaved Americans. The Reconstruction-era additions to the Constitution—the Thirteenth, Fourteenth, and Fifteenth Amendments—enshrined in American law the principles of equality and dignity that had informed abolitionism since the time of Christ.

THE POST-SLAVERY PERIOD

Any belief that the civil rights amendments would settle the matter of equality and justice for ex-slaves and other Black Americans proved to be mistaken. Following Reconstruction, Whites returned to political power in the South and began restoring a system of both legal and extralegal discrimination designed to prevent African Americans from having equal access to the political and economic benefits of

---

[8] Parish, *Slavery*, 1.

[9] Southern apologists for slavery similarly argued that freedom and progress were founded on—not antithetical to—a system of human bondage. See Eugene D. Genovese, *The Slaveholders' Dilemma: Freedom and Progress in Southern Conservative Thought, 1820–1860* (Columbia: University of South Carolina Press, 1992).

American life. By the turn of the twentieth century, institutional segregation ("Jim Crow") pervaded the South and was rampant in the North as well.

Theoretically, the "separate but equal" doctrine articulated by the Supreme Court in the *Plessy v. Ferguson* decision of 1896 guaranteed equivalent resources and opportunities for both White and Black races, but such equality was almost never realized in practice. In South Carolina's Clarendon County, for example, the total value of three schools housing 808 Black children was one-fourth that of the two schools that served 276 White students. The White student to teacher ratio was 28:1 while the Black ratio was 47:1. Per capita spending was $170 per year for White pupils and $43 per year for Black ones.[10]

Jim Crow-style discrimination was not limited to the South. In the North, segregation was less formal and systematic but nonetheless widespread and pernicious. Blacks in the North challenged segregated public schools, where discrepancies similar to those in the South prevailed: schools serving Blacks were overcrowded compared to their White counterparts.[11] Historian Thomas Sugrue summarizes the situation:

> Most northern communities did not erect signs to mark separate Black and White facilities; only some northern schools were segregated by law; and Black voters were not systematically disenfranchised in the North. But in both regions, private behavior, market practices, and public policies created and reinforced racial separation and inequality. Northern Blacks lived as second-class citizens, unencumbered by the most blatant southern-style Jim Crow laws but still trapped in an economic, political, and legal regime that seldom recognized them as equals.[12]

---

[10] Juan Williams, with the *Eyes on the Prize* production team, *Eyes on the Prize: America's Civil Rights Years, 1954–1965* (New York: Viking, 1987), 19, 21.

[11] Thomas J. Sugrue, *Sweet Land of Liberty: The Forgotten Struggle for Civil Rights in the North* (New York: Random House, 2008), chap. 6.

[12] Sugrue, *Sweet Land of Liberty*, xv.

Northern Jim Crow, Sugrue concludes, was "capricious and frustrating," and negotiating it "exhausting, demoralizing, and dangerous."[13]

Early Civil Rights

Post-Reconstruction discrimination and oppression provoked some Blacks to action, with a discernible movement arising in the 1920s and 1930s. As with abolitionism, there continued to be a close connection between Christian activism and civil rights. Anna Arnold Hedgeman, an early activist, "never lost her deep sense of piety, nor her maternalistic belief in the power of uplift." During the 1950s, she was still recommending imitation of "simple, direct, and holy life of Jesus," and criticizing debased culture of "drenched with jump and jive music."[14]

In the North in particular, early civil rights efforts achieved some limited success. Many states had passed laws forbidding separate-but-equal institutions, denial of service to Blacks, and other civil rights violations, and sometimes Black activists and their White allies could use the legal system to their advantage. Combining legal action and moral suasion, activists all but eliminated Jim Crow practices in public theaters in northern cities during the 1920s.[15]

Even so, legal victories for racial rights were few and far between during the early twentieth century, especially in the South. During World War II, African Americans drafted into the armed forces were relegated to second-class status and segregation remained pervasive in the military, even to the point of racially separating blood that was donated for the war effort. Cracks in the racialist edifice appeared during the war, however, as Blacks and some other Americans recognized the untenable tension between the rhetoric of rights as employed in the American war effort against the Axis powers and the reality of the inhumane treatment of large numbers of citizens within the "land of the free." If the United States claimed it was a democratic, free country in contrast to an oppressive, anti-Semitic regime, what about disfranchisement and discrimination against Black Americans? In response to these complaints, President Franklin Roosevelt issued

---

[13] Sugrue, *Sweet Land of Liberty*, 131–32.

[14] Sugrue, *Sweet Land of Liberty*, 21.

[15] Sugrue, *Sweet Land of Liberty*, 133–34, 138–42.

Executive Order 8802 in 1941, forbidding racial discrimination by defense contractors and creating Committee on Fair Employment Practices. Like other early efforts, application of the order was spotty in practice, but it was at least a symbolic step in right direction.[16]

Racial tension remained a constant through the twentieth century, even during the ostensibly uniting experience of World War II and in spite of government gestures. Detroit, where thousands of Blacks moved from the South to get jobs in defense-related industries, was one hotspot. In June 1943, thirty-four people died when Blacks, Whites, and police clashed in a series of violent encounters.[17] In the postwar years, continuing Black dissatisfaction with second-class status would catalyze the early civil-rights efforts into a national movement that would transform the nation.

THE MOVEMENT GAINS STEAM

In 1954, the Supreme Court reversed the *Plessy* decision of fifty-eight years before and ordered the desegregation of American education. This date is commonly viewed as the beginning of the classic civil rights movement, which culminated a decade later with the passage of the Voting Rights Act of 1965.

The Court's decision in *Brown v. Board of Education* was only the beginning of the effort to desegregate schools and other institutions. Southern states initiated painfully slow and incomplete plans to integrate—in many places, in effect, delaying it into an indefinite point in the future. There were tense and sometimes violent battles in places such as Central High School in Little Rock, Arkansas; the University of Alabama in Tuscaloosa; and the University of Mississippi in Oxford—all of which provoked federal intervention.

Beyond education, activists sought equal treatment at lunch counters, on buses, and at the voting booth. The last was perhaps the most contentious of all, as White racists recognized that, with substantial numbers of Blacks voting, they would lack the backing to remain in power and the entire Jim Crow edifice would crumble.

Potential Black voters were intimidated and discriminated against throughout the South, but the nadir of African American political

---

[16] Sugrue, *Sweet Land of Liberty*, 57, 80–82.

[17] Sugrue, *Sweet Land of Liberty*, 68.

life was Mississippi. In the 1950s, 45 percent of the state's population was Black, but only 5 percent of those Blacks were registered to vote. White registrars could arbitrarily judge would-be registrants' ability to "read and interpret" the Mississippi state constitution, a requirement to qualify for the franchise. At times, highly educated Blacks would be turned down by incompetent registrars. In one of the nerve centers of the movements, Selma, Alabama, a Black teacher was failed by the White registrar after the official was embarrassed that the teacher had to help him read the literacy test questionnaire. Despite intense efforts to register Blacks in Mississippi during the late 1950s and early 1960s, the percentage registered increased to only 6.7 percent by 1964, on the cusp of the Voting Rights Act. In Selma, intimidation by White officials such as the notorious Sheriff James Clark meant that just 156 of the city's fifteen thousand eligible Black voters were registered as of 1963.[18]

White intimidation had often succeeded in the past, but the movement of the 1950s and 1960s could not be so easily suppressed. The modest successes achieved in the North became a training ground and inspiration for the southern wing of the movement. Activists such as C. T. Vivian, a prominent figure in the 1960 Nashville sit-ins, had also been involved in restaurant protests in Peoria 1947. The bus segregation pioneer Rosa Parks attended Highlander Folk School in Tennessee, where experienced northern activists taught her the tactics they had perfected elsewhere.[19]

The heyday of the movement brought into existence a panoply of civil rights organizations and raised to prominence a few that had already been active. It did the same for a generation of civil rights leaders. The NAACP, CORE, SCLC, and SNCC were some of the most important groups.[20] The Atlanta-born Martin Luther King Jr., a minister based at Dexter Avenue Baptist Church in Montgomery, Alabama, and president of the SCLC, became the best known of the leaders, but there were many other key figures, including clergy such as Fred Shuttlesworth and Ralph Abernathy; professional activists such as A.

---

[18] Williams, *Eyes on the Prize*, 252, 254.

[19] Sugrue, *Sweet Land of Liberty*, 159–60.

[20] National Association for the Advancement of Colored People (founded 1909); Congress of Racial Equality (1942); Southern Christian Leadership Conference (1957); Student Nonviolent Coordinating Committee (1960).

Philip Randolph and Medgar Evers; student advocates such as John Lewis; professionals such as Roy Wilkins and Thurgood Marshall; and ordinary citizens who became symbols of resistance to oppression, such as Rosa Parks.

While events in Mississippi, Alabama, and Georgia received the lion's share of attention, the movement's northern wing battled on as well. As demographic trends intensified, the plight of Blacks in the North was increasingly important. The 1960 census revealed that 40 percent of Blacks lived outside the South, and that share was growing. It also showed that, for the first time ever, more Blacks than Whites (by percentage of group) lived in urban centers, an effect of massive migration of rural southerners to the urban North.[21]

One of the chief areas of northern attention was the highly seg-regated residential housing market. Efforts to desegregate housing faced an array of obstacles: restrictive covenants (private contracts to exclude Blacks from housing developments); city ordinances that, for example, prohibited Blacks from being out after dark; and federal housing subsidies that reinforced segregation. Even after courts struck down or tempered these measures, extralegal actions and attitudes accomplished the same end—for example, when real estate agents, homeowners, and developers steered or discriminated against pro-spective buyers based on race.[22]

Efforts to integrate neighborhoods often provoked major conflict. In Levittown, Pennsylvania, for example, in 1957, a Black couple that moved in endured crowds of protestors outside their home and had their windows broken and their fire insurance policy canceled. The effort also drew many White supporters, some of whom suffered simi-lar repercussions.[23]

---

[21] Sugrue, *Sweet Land of Liberty*, 255.

[22] Sugrue, *Sweet Land of Liberty*, chap. 7.

[23] Sugrue, *Sweet Land of Liberty*, 220–28.

VICTORY: THE CIVIL RIGHTS ACTS

By the 1960s, the victories of the civil rights movement were accumulating. The decline of discrimination across many parts of the country was evident in the career of *The Negro Motorist Green Book*, which began publication in 1937 as a guide for Blacks to identify safe motels and restaurants when traveling. *Green Book* sales declined in the 1950s as the situation improved, and with Jim Crow on its deathbed, it ceased publication in 1964.[24]

The demise of Jim Crow marked the apogee of the civil rights movement, as two monumental bills were passed in succession: the Civil Rights Act of 1964 and the Voting Rights Act of 1965. The former prohibited discrimination in public accommodations, facilities, and schools; outlawed discrimination in federally funded projects; created the Equal Employment Opportunity Commission to monitor employment discrimination in public and private sectors; and provided additional capacities to enforce voting rights. The Voting Rights Act suspended the use of literacy tests and voter disqualification devices for five years; authorized the use of federal examiners to supervise voter registration in states that used tests or in which less than half the voting-eligible residents registered or voted; directed the US attorney general to institute proceedings against the use of poll taxes; and provided criminal penalties for individuals who violated the act.[25] With the passage of these laws, a firm basis was finally in place to ensure the legal and political rights of Black Americans.

The effect was real change. "Immediately upon its passage," historian Allen Matusow recounts, the 1964 law brought an end to denials of service to Blacks at gas stations, restaurants, and motels across most of the urban South. There was also considerable success in the field of voting rights. In the six states targeted by the act, voter registration increased from 31 percent to 57 percent of the eligible Black population in three years; in Alabama, from 19 percent to 53 percent, and

---

[24] Sugrue, *Sweet Land of Liberty*, 160.

[25] These summaries are taken from the chart "Constitutional Amendments and Major Civil Rights Acts of Congress Referenced in Black Americans in Congress," located at History, Art & Archives, United States House of Representatives, https://history.house.gov/Exhibitions-and-Publications/BAIC/Historical-Data/Constitutional-Amendments-and-Legislation/.

in Mississippi from 6 percent to 44 percent.[26] This improvement was matched by dramatic shifts in public opinion. Whereas in 1944 only 45 percent of Whites polled agreed that "Negroes should have as good a chance as Whites to get any kind of job," by 1963 agreement had risen 35 points to 80 percent.[27]

UNIVERSAL APPEAL

The change in American law and culture between 1954 and 1965 was dramatic. One of the keys to understanding the civil rights movement's success is its capacity to embrace a wide variety of Americans. The movement, although almost always propelled and populated predominantly by African Americans, always enjoyed some White support—varying from tepid to vigorous depending on the time and place. Early figures such as William Lloyd Garrison, John Brown, and Lyman Beecher are well known; there were also many obscure but important collaborators in the underground railroad and other efforts to assist slaves and ex-slaves.[28] This White support continued and crescendoed through the heyday of the movement in the 1960s.

In a majority-White nation, it was inevitable that the movement must obtain support from at least some percentage of the White population. This was part of the reason that most of its leadership was committed to peaceful protest (in addition to, for some, principled commitment to nonviolence). Civil rights activists were thus compelled to perform a delicate dance: Push hard enough to challenge the persuadable portion of the White majority to abandon their positions of skepticism or indifference toward the plight of Blacks, but do not push so hard so fast that moderate Whites turn against the movement out of fear of radicalism or concern for public order. Movement leaders avoided charges of radicalism not only by adhering to nonviolence but also by appealing to ideals that were broadly shared by all Americans. The inalienable rights of the Declaration of Independence—life, liberty,

---

[26] Allen Matusow, *The Unraveling of America: A History of Liberalism in the 1960s* (New York: Harper and Row, 1984), 187–88.

[27] Matusow, *Unraveling of America*, 211.

[28] See, for example, Eric Foner, *Gateway to Freedom: The Hidden History of the Underground Railroad* (New York: W. W. Norton & Company, 2015).

and the pursuit of happiness—were at the core of the civil rights movement and figured prominently in its rhetoric.

This common-ground approach to civil rights was abetted by the movement's close ties to Christianity. The success that the movement did achieve depended in large measure on its appeal to the conscience of a White majority—an appeal that could have no effect if both groups (Black civil rights spokesmen and White sympathizers) did not share a common set of moral principles—that is, a fundamentally Judeo-Christian worldview. Black clergy figured prominently in the movement, and religious language suffused its parlance. The crucial role of religion is on display in the most prominent of its figures, the Reverend Martin Luther King Jr.

Religion was one influence in generating the heroic nonviolence that characterized King and so many other civil rights activists. As the historian Christopher Lasch explains, Blacks in the South in the 1950s "had every reason to sink into cynicism and despair, to accept exploitation passively, or on the other hand to throw themselves into a politics of resentment and revenge." Instead, in the civil rights movement in the South, "the 'spiritual discipline against resentment' flowered in its purest form." "Having grown up under an intolerably oppressive system of race relations," King "understood the equally dangerous temptations of acquiescence and revenge."[29]

Eminent civil rights historians have affirmed the wisdom of King's approach. John Hope Franklin recognized how "difficult" it has been for Blacks to subsist in a violent American culture "without becoming infected with the virus of violence." Yet acceding to violence, he concluded, has not been fruitful. Beyond the danger of alienating potential White sympathizers with their cause, Black internalization of violence had a pernicious effect within the Black community itself. "The tragedy was that all too often Blacks turned their hostility and frustration toward the larger society inward, not in terms of peace, but in terms of violence, bringing heartbreak and suffering down on their own families and neighbors."[30] Richard H. King affirmed the conciliatory approach as well: "Forgiving and forgetting would not

---

[29] Christopher Lasch, *The True and Only Heaven: Progress and Its Critics* (New York: W. W. Norton, 1991), 387, 393.

[30] John Hope Franklin, "Martin Luther King, Jr., and the Afro-American Protest Tradition," in *We Shall Overcome: Martin Luther King, Jr., and the*

be ways for Black Americans to excuse what had been done to them. They would, rather, free Black Americans from the embittering force of remembered suffering and injustice."[31]

King's capacity to resist temptations to resentment and violence was built on a sophisticated theological base. King encountered the writings of the eminent Social Gospel minister Walter Rauschenbusch at Crozer Seminary 1948. Rauschenbusch, King attested, "left an indelible imprint on my thinking by giving me a theological basis for the social concern which had already grown up in me as a result of my early experiences." But King differed with Rauschenbusch's "cult of inevitable progress," which "led him to a superficial optimism concerning man's nature" and "came perilously close to identifying the Kingdom of God with a particular social and economic system—a tendency which should never befall the Church."[32] The corrective to social gospel optimism was Christian realism. King's study of the Christian theologian Reinhold Niebuhr, Lasch points out, furnished King with a realistic conception of "man's potential for evil."[33] White consciousness of injustice could be raised, but White hostility would also remain. The strategy and conduct of the movement must be formed and proceed within this ambivalent environment.

King's view of forgiveness was radical and empowering. "Forgiveness does not mean ignoring what has been done or putting a false label on an evil act. It means, rather, that the evil act no longer remains as a barrier to the relationship." He insisted that "the evil deed of the enemy-neighbor, the thing that hurts, never quite expresses all that he is. An element of goodness may be found even in our worst enemy." For King, these challenging but powerful ideas were rooted in the gospel, in the words of Jesus in Matthew 5:43–45. He concluded,

---

Black Freedom Struggle, ed. Peter J. Albert and Ronald Hoffman (New York: Pantheon, 1990), 109.

[31] Richard H. King, "Martin Luther King, Jr., and the Meaning of Freedom: A Political Interpretation," in *We Shall Overcome,* 152.

[32] King, "Pilgrimage to Nonviolence," chap. 3 in *The Radical King,* ed. Cornel West (Boston: Beacon Press, 2015), 40; previously published as a chapter in *Stride Toward Freedom* (1958) and as an article in *Christian Century* (1960).

[33] Lasch, *True and Only Heaven,* 386–90.

"Love even for enemies is the key to the solution of the problems of our world."[34]

Reliance on his faith was more than an intellectual exercise for King; it was a critical support during the tribulations the movement underwent. At times, King struggled to persevere in the face of violent and perverse threats against himself and his family. During the Montgomery bus boycott in January of 1956, he was "ready to give up" and "decided to take my problem to God." Having confessed his weariness and discouragement,

> At that moment I experienced the presence of the Divine as I had never experienced Him before. It seemed as though I could hear the quiet assurance of an inner voice saying: "Stand up for righteousness, stand up for truth; and God will be at your side forever." Almost at once my fears began to go. My uncertainty disappeared. I was ready to face anything.[35]

The qualities modeled by King and adopted by a large portion of the movement did in fact attract large numbers of White sympathizers and, sometimes, active collaborators. In the movement's early experiments in desegregating restaurants in the North, it enjoyed cooperation from Whites who acted as "testers" (to gauge whether treatment of Blacks and Whites was consistent) and as witnesses. White cooperators, such as Clifford and Virginia Durr during the Montgomery bus boycott, risked economic and social backlash and worse. White freedom rider Jim Zwerg was viciously attacked during a melee in Birmingham in May 1961. Andrew Goodman and Michael Schwerner were murdered in 1964 while assisting the Black voter and registration drive of Freedom Summer in Mississippi (1964). James Reeb, a Unitarian minister, was killed in Selma during the unrest of 1965. White lawyers and journalists played vital roles in the movement's legal and public relations campaigns. Finally, the movement also had allies in the Whites-dominated halls of government. An all-White

---

[34] Martin Luther King Jr., "Loving Your Enemies," in *The Radical King*, ed. Cornel West (Boston: Beacon Press, 2015; originally published in *Strength to Love*, 1963), 56–57.

[35] Martin Luther King Jr., *Stride Toward Freedom: The Montgomery Story* (New York: Harper, 1958), 134.

Supreme Court issued the *Brown* decision, unanimously. Presidents Eisenhower, Kennedy, and Johnson, often less than zealous advocates of Black rights, nonetheless aided the cause by backing desegregation and voting rights with federal force at crucial points.[36]

The civil rights movement, which began as a small, Black-initiated effort to counter discrimination against Blacks in particular locales, grew into a nationwide, broadly supported campaign to align de facto and de jure treatment of Blacks with the stated principles of the American political system. That goal, rhetorically connected to and genuinely consistent with core American values and Judeo-Christian mores, could and did appeal to a wide array of Americans across political, racial, and religious boundaries.[37]

FISSURES

Any social or political movement develops and exhibits division, and the civil rights movement was no exception. From the beginning, abolition advocates differed in their tactics, ranging from violent rebellion to immediate extralegal action to legal political activity. After Reconstruction, differing ideas among Blacks themselves about how best to advance within a hostile society were epitomized in the dispute between Booker T. Washington (moral propriety, educational attainment, and economic success) and W. E. B. DuBois (political activism and insistence on legal rights).

As early as the 1930s, some activists saw civil rights as part of a broader campaign of economic reform. A. Philip Randolph sought to link economic welfare—meaning a particular policy program—with

---

[36] Sugrue, *Sweet Land of Liberty*, 142–54; Williams, *Eyes on the Prize*, 82–83, 155, chap. 7, 275.

[37] This discussion of the "universality" of the movement's appeal is not intended to imply that there remained no opposition, even strident opposition, to the movement in general or specific pieces of the civil rights agenda in particular. Although Martin Luther King was a relatively "unifying" figure amid the balkanizing 1960s, polling at the time reveals that many Americans— Black and White, for various reasons—had negative views of him. See Frank Newport, "Martin Luther King Jr.: Revered More After Death Than Before," Gallup, January 16, 2006, https://news.gallup.com/poll/20920/martin-luther-king-jr-revered-more-after-death-than-before.aspx.

civil rights. "What had been a marginal position among civil rights activists—that class and race were intertwined, that jobs were necessary for freedom, that unionism was a prerequisite to civil rights—moved to the center of the Black freedom struggle."[38] But this move was problematic, because it assumed that a leftist economic program was the equivalent of racial equality. The claim marginalized any potential Black or White collaborators who might be sympathetic to Black political rights but dissent from left-leaning economic policy.

Although remarkable cooperation was achieved during the critical years of the 1950s and 1960s, differences along the continuums from radicalism to gradualism and from confrontation to collaboration continued to exist throughout the twentieth century. Younger, more militant leaders led the push toward the civil disobedience of sit-ins and freedom rides, differing with the older generation's focus on working through the court system.[39] While Martin Luther King, a preacher dressed in suit and tie and speaking polished English, presented an image and message that White America could accept, more radical elements such as Malcolm X, the Black Panthers, and the Nation of Islam displayed a facet of the movement that more Whites found alien and frightening—and that most Blacks also rejected.

After the political victories at the pinnacle of the movement in the mid-1960s, these divisions deepened and the clarity of the movement's direction was lost in a haze of changing movement objectives and national priorities—preeminently the divisive conflict in Vietnam. For a segment of the movement, the end of legally enforced desegregation and disfranchisement did not represent the end of the fight. Economic equality must be achieved as well, and that could only happen, they thought, through a fundamental transformation of the American economic system. This opened the door to substantial Marxist influence.

The relationship between civil rights and socialism and communism already had a long and complicated past. In the 1920s and 1930s, labor groups, socialists, and communists had been among the small minority of Whites who took strong stands for Black rights.[40] Although few

---

[38] Sugrue, *Sweet Land of Liberty*, 34.

[39] Williams, *Eyes on the Prize*, chap. 5.

[40] Sugrue, *Sweet Land of Liberty*, 22–26.

Blacks were themselves socialistic in their economic thinking, they found common cause with Communists on this issue and enjoyed a friendly political alliance.[41]

There were persistent differences, too, between those who supported King's cooperative approach and those who advocated Black self-assertion. In the early 1960s, the Reverend Albert Cleage Jr. of Detroit disavowed the civil rights establishment, such as King and the NAACP, as "Uncle Toms." Cleage disdained alliance with White liberals and stressed Black self-determination. This rift was evident during a July 1963 rally in Chicago, where the crowd booed not only Mayor Daley as an unwelcome White collaborator, but also the Reverend Joseph H. Jackson, head of the National Baptist Convention and a critic of Black radicalism.[42] Although King remains a towering figure in both popular and academic understandings of the movement, his leadership was not unquestioned, unequivocal, or even indispensable in many instances.[43]

The prevalence of division in the midst of victory was also evident in reaction to the Moynihan Report (1965). Released by assistant secretary of labor and future Democratic Senator Daniel Patrick Moynihan, the report was a good-faith attempt to diagnose the causes of differentials in White and Black socioeconomic measures. Moynihan praised the success of the civil rights movement and applauded the legal equality achieved, but he also presciently warned that the dysfunctions evident in a large section of Black family life promised to derail continued economic and social progress. Reaction foreshadowed the conflict to come. Some Black leaders agreed with the analysis, recognizing that the continuing decline of Black fatherhood, for example, would imperil the educational and vocational achievement of Black youth. Others, however, attacked the report as White meddling in internal

---

[41] See, for example, the discussion of pioneering civil rights lawyer Charles Hamilton Houston in Genna Rae McNeill, *Groundwork: Charles Hamilton Houston and the Struggle for Civil Rights* (Philadelphia: University of Pennsylvania Press, 1983), chap. 9.

[42] Sugrue, *Sweet Land of Liberty*, 300, 302.

[43] See, for example, Clayborne Carson, "Reconstructing the King Legacy: Scholars and National Myths," in *We Shall Overcome*, 239–48. Carson points out that "the Black struggle was a locally-based mass movement rather than simply a reform movement led by national civil rights leaders" (245).

Black affairs, as a failure to understand the unique character of the Black family, or as an exercise in "blaming the victim."[44] Thus were set the lines of combat in the ongoing and largely unproductive discussion of race in America that would characterize the next five decades.

THE LATER MOVEMENT

After 1965, the civil rights movement went into eclipse. Some of the reasons were external, as other issues arose that absorbed the nation's attention: Vietnam, the War on Poverty, the sexual revolution, and economic recession. Other reasons were internal. With its major political aims achieved, the internecine tensions already described came to the fore. In 1986, activist Julian Bond wrote of the classic movement that its "philosophy had been one of nonviolence and commitment to achieving change within the American system of law. After 1965, that vision became clouded. The post-1965 rage of Black militants and the fires that their anger left burning across America's cities sometimes obscure the glory of the movement's earlier years."[45] The movement's universal appeal was weakened both by this division—which carried with it an increasing prominence for radical elements—and by the growing identification of civil rights with policies advocated by the political left.

The increasing politicization of civil rights was partially a function of ideology and partially a function of practical reality, the two mutually reinforcing each other. In 1960, NAACP activist Gloster Current called the federal government "the largest civil rights organization today." The basis for this claim extended beyond Supreme Court decisions, legislation, and federal agencies' enforcement of anti-discrimination law. "Over the course of the 1960s," Thomas Sugrue observes, "government became the single most important employer of African Americans in northern cities." In 1970, 20 percent of Blacks were employed by government, including 72 percent of college-educated Black women and 57 percent of college-educated Black men.[46] Increasingly, Black progress became identified with the fortunes of

---

[44] Matusow, *Unraveling of America*, 194–98.

[45] Julian Bond, Introduction, *Eyes on the Prize*, xiv.

[46] Sugrue, *Sweet Land of Liberty*, 398.

government. Concurrently, the Democratic Party became known as the party of "big government," while the Republican Party was the home of "limited government" conservatives. In this environment, it was natural for many Blacks to identify their welfare with the continued expansion of government, and thus to gravitate toward the political left.

PROBLEMS AND PROGRESS

In the decades since 1965, the persistence of both progress and problems among Black Americans has been evident. The growth of the Black middle class is undeniable. In Michigan, for example, in 1960 there were 324 Black doctors, 142 lawyers, 201 engineers, and 95 college teachers. In 1990 there were 1,076 doctors, 1,178 lawyers, 2,658 engineers, and 1,509 college teachers.[47] Black Americans have been elected across the country, representing North and South, to the halls of Congress, and they have been appointed to the Supreme Court. In 2008, Barack Obama was elected to the nation's highest political office, an event that would have been impossible to imagine in 1965.

At the same time, the median income of Blacks lags that of Whites. Black people are disproportionately represented in the ranks of the poor, the unemployed, and the imprisoned. Compared to other racial groups, their life expectancy and educational achievement are lower, and their rates of out-of-wedlock births and abortions are higher.[48] Providing economic opportunity and ensuring sound social structures for Black Americans remain urgent tasks.

To address these problems, contemporary civil rights leaders and a majority of Black politicians continue to advocate increased government intervention. Many civil rights organizations are increas-

---

[47] Sugrue, *Sweet Land of Liberty*, 537.

[48] These and other statistics are reported in R. Kelley Raley, Megan M. Sweeney, and Danielle Wondra, "The Growing Ethnic and Racial Divide in U.S. Marriage Patterns," US National Library of Medicine, National Institutes of Health. Published in final form in *The Future of Children* 25, no. 2 (Fall 2015): 89–109, https://www.ncbi.nlm.nih.gov/pmc/articles/PMC4850739/; and Patrick F. Fagan and Christina Hadford, "The State of the Black Family in America," Marriage and Religion Research Institute, February 2015, http://marri.us/wp-content/uploads/The-State-of-the-Black-Family-in-America.pdf.

ingly critical of traditional American values, employing anti-American rhetoric that denigrates the founding generation, the Constitution, and the American system of government. Some popular groups, such as Black Lives Matter, forthrightly embrace socialist or Marxist economic programs. "Structural racism," in the view of these leaders, infects American life so completely that a complete demolition and rebuilding is necessary. Whites, incapable of eradicating the racism that is intrinsic to their being, are called only to abject apology and obeisance, not to collaboration as fellow human beings made in the image of God or allies in the quest for the equality and justice that were built into the nation's founding documents but are always imperfectly realized.[49]

The classic civil rights movement achieved real success and genuine progress by pursuing a very different path. The half-century since 1965 has, in large measure, been a departure from that path, one that has been less successful. The well-being of future Black Americans—and all Americans—depends to a substantial degree on whether the imprudence of that detour is recognized and the quest for civil rights returns to a more fruitful track.

---

[49] Other chapters in this book supply details concerning the dominant contemporary approaches to civil rights.

2

THEORIES OF RACE*

Ismael Hernandez

The trans-Saharan slave trade dates to the second century AD, and fully functioning slave markets abounded for centuries in various parts of the world. However, slavery had largely died out in Europe until its resurgence during the era of discovery and colonization that saw the Portuguese establish the first Atlantic sugar plantations in Madeira (1455) and the Canary Islands (1496). The labor system instituted in those places served as a model for the New World's sugar plantation system. Brazil was the first transatlantic destination for African slaves, who arrived there in 1538, and later the despicable slave ship brought 350 slaves to Jamestown in 1619.[1]

---

* A version of this chapter was previously published at www.1776unites .com.

[1] R. W. Beachey, *The Slave Trade of Eastern Africa* (London: Rex Collings, 1976), 189–91; Frederick Cooper, *Plantation Slavery on the East Coast of Africa* (New Haven: Yale University Press, 1977), 12; Philip Curtin, *The Rise and Fall of the Plantation Complex: Essays in Atlantic History* (Cambridge: Cambridge University Press, 1998), 4–26; William Phillips Jr. and Carla Rahn Phillips, *The Worlds of Christopher Columbus* (Cambridge: Cambridge University Press, 1992), 52–69; Mark Johnston, "The Sugar Trade in the West Indies and Brazil Between 1492 and 1700," University of Minnesota Libraries, accessed November 3, 2020 (link no longer operational), https://www.lib.umn.edu

Much has already been said about that dreadful event in Jamestown. If we attempt to understand the struggles of race in America from that date on, we must not only look at the antecedent factors often lying just beneath the surface of these events but also at the narratives within which they are embedded. These narratives or filters are often presented as conferring epistemic privilege for some and epistemic blinders for others. For that reason, it is important to understand these constructs. There are two major narratives of race that ought to claim our attention.

RACE IN HISTORY

Before we examine these two narratives, let us quickly glance at the larger question of race in history. The very concept of race seems to be a fuzzy category, lacking clear biological classification. Race as a biological phenomenon is subjective and does not represent a definite category in nature. Instead, race exists as part of a continuum with arbitrary boundaries that are socially construed. As Thomas Sowell states,

> If race were conceived of in purely biological terms, it would be a concept that could be applied to only a relatively hand-ful of people on a few small isolated islands in the oceans.... What are called "races" in this context are simply groups of people with substantially differing proportions of genes from various racial stocks.[2]

Starting in the early part of the seventeenth century, several developments occurred that generated the modern concept of race. Among these factors was Western exploration, ignited in part by mercantilism and the discovery and colonization of new peoples, which brought cultures closer together and made human differences more appar-

/bell/tradeproducts/sugar#n2; Niall Ferguson, *Civilization: The West and the Rest* (New York: Penguin Press, 2011), 130. The experience in the Canaries not only served as a model for plantation-style sugar cane harvesting in the Americas but also as a model for the treatment of slaves both as laborers and commodities.

[2] Thomas Sowell, *The Economics and Politics of Race: An International Perspective* (New York: Morrow & Co., 1983), 16.

ent. The popularization of Darwinism, along with the related though distinct emergence of the theory of Social Darwinism later in the nineteenth century, is another important factor. Darwinists were the first to attempt to bestow on racism some semblance of scientific validity. It is interesting that the subtitle of Darwin's *Origin of the Species* (1859) was *The Preservation of Favoured Races in the Struggle for Life.*

With these influences and the human propensity to parochialism, it was to be expected that people sought answers in a theory of race to questions such as why certain people possess what seem to be inferior cultures. Of course, inferiority is in the eye of the beholder, and the aforementioned parochialism tends to lead us to place ourselves at the pinnacle of civilization. In fact, anthropologists have shown that some of the most primitive tribes embraced myths that placed their tiny groups at the center of the universe.[3]

With the Darwinist insistence on a hierarchy of survival enthroned as a tenet of science, the ideological framework was in place for a rationalization of racial domination. If the question of who is "superior" is asked, the questioner will often find an obvious answer: "Well, we are, of course!" Classifications came with a vengeance under Darwinian influence. The age of exploration, mercantilism, trade, and Darwinism gave a new twist of justification to an ancient institution: slavery. Rivalries among the European powers created a voracious appetite for cash crops and new sources of precious materials, and the need for manpower harvest the bounty. There was powerful demand for a theoretical justification for chattel slavery.

As we know, slavery was ancient and universal. Sociologist Orlando Patterson tells us that "slaveholding and trading existed among the earliest and most primitive of peoples. The archaeological evidence reveals that slaves were among the first items of trade within, and between, the primitive Germans and Celts, and the institution was an established part of life." Virtually as ancient as civilization itself,

---

[3] The purpose of myths has always been to provide an understanding of common origins that strengthens social cohesion. Through sacred narratives that explain the origin of the world, the universe, mankind, and the events leading to the present situation of the group, clans found a way to answer existential questions. These myths were often expressed through rituals and stories couched in simple, unambiguous terms, to convey religious or idealized experiences that offered meaning and purpose.

slavery existed in Africa, China, Japan, and the prehistoric Near East. Hunter gatherers in North America practiced it. The North American Cherokees practiced slavery, with slaves being the *atsi nahsa'i*, or people without rights or participation in social life. Their main purpose was to serve as an anomaly, pointing to the strength and unity of the Cherokees as a group.[4]

However, in Europe there was another important influence: Christianity. Eventually the Christian West not only questioned slavery but birthed a movement to end it. Under the influence of religious groups such as the Quakers, by the end of the eighteenth-century slavery seemed intolerable; in 1807 Great Britain abolished its slave trade and fifteen years later France followed suit. These accomplishments occurred despite strong opposition from most of the non-Western world. African tribal leaders in Gambia, Congo, and Dahomey (Nigeria) sent delegations to London and Paris to lobby against ending the slave trade, and intra-African trade in slaves grew exponentially after the Europeans ended their participation.[5]

The quest to abolish slavery extended to America, although it took longer to achieve here, mostly due to economic reasons. The antebellum South evolved into a segmented economy heavily dependent on agriculture, with an aristocratic elite benefiting from slave labor. It is important to note that Darwinian biological theories were not the impetus for Blacks' enslavement; they were enslaved for economic reasons. Slavery was later rationalized using various theories, including the Darwinian, which became prevalent only after the paternalistic religious rationalization began to falter.[6] Because slavery in many places had become a racialized institution, theories of racial superiority were invented to justify its continuation. Thus, even after slavery was

---

[4] Orlando Patterson, *Freedom in the Making of Western Culture* (New York: Basic Books, 1991), 11; Thomas Sowell, *Race and Culture: A World View* (New York: Basic Books, 1995), 186; Thomas Sowell, *Conquests and Cultures: An International History* (New York: Basic Books, 1998), 109; Theda Perdue, *Society, Slavery and the Evolution of Cherokee, 1540–1866* (Knoxville: University of Tennessee Press, 1979), chap. 1.

[5] John Perazzo, *The Myths That Divide Us* (New York: World Studies Books, 1999), 372–74.

[6] See George Frederickson, *White Supremacy* (Oxford: Oxford University Press, 1981), 76–85.

legally outlawed, those theories were still potent weapons of justification for efforts to maintain the economic and political dominance of some races over others. This explains why Darwinism, which emerged only as systematic slavery was in its death throes, remained a vital component of racialist thought.

In any event, our history was imbued with a binary reality: a country founded on the idea of freedom still had within itself a racialized institution that contradicted the goals of liberty. With this background in place, we can now discuss the two streams or narratives of thought used to explain the American race problem.

THE PERSONALIST NARRATIVE

The first stream is one I call the Personalist/Integrationist Approach (PIA). It is important to note in addressing this stream of thought that America benefited from the idea of individual freedom as an institutional value, which only took hold in the Christian West. As the sociologist Orlando Patterson tell us, "While the idea of freedom was certainly engendered wherever slavery existed, it never came to term. People everywhere, except in the West, resisted its gestation and institutionalization."[7]

In non-Western societies, and for a period also in the West, the slave dreamed of becoming socially born-again by recapturing acceptable social dependency. That dependency was his only hope, as full citizenship after being released from slavery was seldom attained.[8] Personal freedom as we understand it was denied not only to the slave but to all members of tribal societies, as all relationships were dependent on the community. In effect, it is in the relationship between the slave and the "freeman" that we find the essence of the idea of freedom in the non-Western world—the freeman's liberty consisting of full integration within the kin group rather than individual liberty. In the absence of the possibility of individual independence, there was a more practical goal for non-Westerners: that of fully belonging to the group for some and, for the slave, the reduction of marginality by regaining corporate status socially, legally, and ritualistically.

---

[7] Patterson, *Freedom in the Making*, 20.

[8] Patterson, *Freedom in the Making*, 22–23.

This regaining of corporate status was to be accomplished by escaping or by attempting the often-unsuccessful task of being welcomed within the clan of the slave's captors. There was social capital in being a member of the tribe, and often the slave was a kind of social currency and token of recognition of the value of integration, a reminder for the tribe that the members were not like the slave and that unity within the group brought about safety from the dreaded fate the slave exemplified. The free-slave dichotomy did not obtain in the non-Western world because all social status was involuntary and subordinated to the community.

In the PIA understanding of race that informed the earlier stages of the civil rights movement, the person, the individual, has a status different from what was conceived by the non-Western mind. Ethnic identity is seen as an aspect of the larger reality of individual personhood. Through a long and interesting historical process magnificently recounted by Orlando Patterson in his seminal *Freedom in the Making of Western Culture,* the Western mind conceived an alternative of social existence that was neither isolation and social death nor subordination to the group. Personal freedom was eventually conceived and actualized. A series of revolutions in ancient Athens transformed the Western world in a way that allowed for the social construction of freedom as a central value.[9] This central value became a preoccupation for Greek philosophy and later for the Christian natural law tradition via its connection to Aristotelian thought. Roman power expanded this idea both in geographical terms, through conquest and rule, and in social terms, concerning who could aspire to it, as they co-opted the leadership of allied states. Through compromise and strategic maneuverings for power, freedom was indirectly expanded to others. Christianity, in effect, moved this journey toward its institutional-

---

[9] Patterson, *Freedom in the Making,* chap. 3. The five revolutions described by Patterson are the creation of a preindustrial economy of independent family farms; the emergence of a large slave population who sustained the lives of the aristocracy, combined with the emergence of a non-slave population economically emancipated from the elites; the invention of Greek democracy; the emergence of Greek philosophy; and the final construction of individual freedom as a realizable central value.

ization.[10] The possibility of autonomy against the threat of dreadful slavery obtained in this environment, whereas only fusion within the kin group emerged as a practical alternative in the non-Western world.

The Western mind thus arrived at autonomy through a long struggle that was in many ways parasitic to the very existence of slavery. Personalists believe that the founders of our nation were for the most part successful in suffusing our founding documents with universal natural law principles of individual human dignity consistent with the Western development of the idea of individual freedom. Whatever one might think of the arrival of slaves in 1619, its significance is filtered through the prism of the understanding of freedom expressed in the documents of 1776 and the Western discovery of individual freedom. The existence of contradiction on the ground of experience is to be expected in a process that, as we have detailed, saw human beings at the crossroads of various influences.

Adherents to this stream believe that the American constitutional framework could, over time, overcome social, economic, and political racial stratification and expand the realm of freedom. Embedded in the founding principles of the Constitution was the seed of the solution to the problem, even if that solution required a long and often arduous journey. The Constitution was not perfect, but neither was it fatally flawed. Its basic principle was not White supremacy but liberty.[11]

The 1960s civil rights movement was grounded in the belief that Black integration was a right, a social good, and a real possibility. Just as Westerners over time discovered that the dichotomy of social death or collectivist integration was false because there was another option, the movement thrust ahead, albeit in the face of great struggle, by

---

[10] Patterson, *Freedom in the Making*, 204–7, and part 4. It should be noted that another important factor in the development of the Western notion of freedom is that, although Rome's economy during the middle and late Republic was based heavily on slave labor, free farmers and workers were never eliminated as a supplementary labor force. In this contrast and in the many contradictions and oppressive realities of the time, the seed of liberty as autonomy took hold. By the fifth century BC, the Roman concept of freedom, *libertas*, was roughly identical to ours. See pages 219–22.

[11] See Timothy Sandefur, *The Conscience of the Constitution: The Declaration of Independence and the Right to Liberty* (Washington, DC: Cato Institute, 2014), chap. 1.

rejecting the social death or separation alternative. Dr. Martin Luther King's "Letter from a Birmingham Jail" is probably the best expression of this view. "Be true to what you say on paper!" was his insistent cry.[12]

The antithesis to the slavery system brought to our shores as human cargo in 1619 was freedom in the Western sense: freedom to a group of people destined to recreate themselves in a foreign land that became their own—a people destined to be the quintessential Americans who forged an existential reality in the midst of isolation from their past and the imposed degradation of their present. Partial resocialization within the master's community was not destiny but a step on a journey of full integration informed by the value of freedom. Reform is possible, however searing conditions might seem at a given time, if there is historical evidence that positive changes can occur based on the substantive set of principles that inform a system. The arrival of slave cargo ships in 1619 was the background against which the story of a people was forged based on the principles of liberty carved in 1776. Slavery was scenery in the drama of a new people of destiny.[13]

If this is true, the heart of the PIA understanding of race in America can be said to be *optimism*. This optimism is neither without justification nor without caution, knowing well that the emergence of freedom in history was never without travails. Optimism is possible because the philosophical foundations of the Constitution, benefiting from the slow and tortuous discovery of individual freedom in the Western mind, demonstrated that it is possible to expand its reach to cover more and more classes of people.[14] In other words, this stream was

---

[12] Martin Luther King, Jr., "I've Been to the Mountaintop," April 3, 1968. American Rhetoric: Top 100 Speeches, https://www.americanrhetoric.com/speeches/mlkivebeentothemountaintop.htm.

[13] A good historical discussion of Blacks as quintessential Americans is found in Alan Keyes, *Masters of the Dream: The Strength and Betrayal of Black America* (New York: William Morrow, 1995).

[14] Lily Ross Taylor, *Party Politics in the Age of Caesar* (Berkeley: University of California Press, 1949), chaps. 1, 2, and 5; Patterson, *Freedom in the Making*, 222–23. One chapter in the story of freedom can showcase such practical possibility. During the first century BC, we see a development in the Roman mind away from virtue understood genetically, involving bloodlines, to virtue (*virtus*) based on personal achievement in competition. Of course, this cultural emphasis did not bring about immediate equality or an expansion of

integrationist, reformist, and *optimistic,* while recognizing the reality of sin, and this aligns it with philosophical realism.[15]

This optimism is complemented by the Christian expansion of salvation to the gentiles. The gentiles were called to the church and, as the church and the state drew closer and the power of Rome backed the church, liberties were expanded from the kin group to the nations. The very distortions of biblical exegesis used by some to justify enslavement demonstrates that in the Western and Christian mind there needed to be a way to accommodate action to biblical principles that pointed in the direction of freedom. There was a psychological and intellectual need to find a way to deal with the ideas of liberty found in biblical stories. Moreover, the adherents to this stream espoused the same conviction shared by John Adams and many other Founders: that general, immutable, and unalterable Christian and natural law principles informed the meaning of law in the American constitutional understanding of governance.[16] As Martin Luther King often

---

democracy beyond the male aristocratic elite, but it moved the lever further toward a new understanding of *libertas.*

[15] Alexander Miller, "Realism," *The Stanford Encyclopedia of Philosophy* (Winter 2019 Edition), ed. Edward Zalta, https://plato.stanford.edu/archives/win2019/entries/realism/. "There are two general aspects to realism, illustrated by looking at realism about the everyday world of macroscopic objects and their properties. First, there is a claim about *existence.* Tables, rocks, the moon, and so on, all exist, as do the following facts: the table's being square, the rock's being made of granite, and the moon's being spherical and yellow. The second aspect of realism about the everyday world of macroscopic objects and their properties concerns *independence.* The fact that the moon exists and is spherical is independent of anything anyone happens to say or think about the matter."

[16] In a letter to Thomas Jefferson concerning the revolutionary principles, John Adams says,

> And what were these principles? I answer, the general principles of Christianity in which all those sects were united and the general principles of English and American liberty in which all these young men united.... Now I will avow that I then believe and now believe that those general principles of Christianity are as eternal and immutable as the existence and attributes of God. And that those principles of liberty are as unalterable as human nature.

repeated, a law lacks character as true law when it is unjust and violates the eternal moral law, and it must be disobeyed precisely because it violates the principles of the Constitution.[17] His philosophy was deeply personalist.[18] Natural law is a finite reflection of the infinite wisdom of God, and human law must conform with this reflection.[19] In a sense, natural law gives this stream of thought an adherence to universal truths about the human person as a *point of departure* to understand social reality. The human person, unique and unrepeatable, with the moral capacities of reason and volition, stands *sui generis* in the midst of the group, whose well-being does not supersede the dignity embedded in the person but is called to respect that dignity in view of the common good.[20]

"John Adams to Thomas Jefferson, 28 June 1813," Founders Online, National Archives, https://founders.archives.gov/documents/Jefferson/03-06-02 -0208.

[17] Martin Luther King Jr., "Letter from a Birmingham Jail," April 16, 1963, African Studies Center, University of Pennsylvania, https://www.africa.upenn. edu/Articles_Gen/Letter_Birmingham.html. In his words: "A just law is a man-made code that squares with the moral law or the law of God. An unjust law is a code that is out of harmony with the moral law." See Thomas Aquinas, *Summa Theologiae* I–II, q. 91, a. 1, for Aquinas's understanding of the eternal law.

[18] King followed the personalism of his Boston University teacher and mentor, Edgard S. Brightman, who was associated with the Boston Personalist movement. "Personalism's insistence that only personality—finite and infinite—is ultimately real, strengthened me in two convictions. It gave me metaphysical and philosophical grounding for the idea of a personal God, and it gave me a metaphysical basis for the dignity and worth of all human personality." Martin Luther King, Jr., *Stride Toward Freedom* (New York: Harper & Row, 1958), 100.

[19] See J. Budziszewski, *Written on the Heart: The Case for Natural Law* (Downers Grove: InterVarsity Press, 1997), 56–57. Aquinas defines human law as "an ordinance of reason, for the common good, made by him who has care of the community, and promulgated." *Summa Theologiae*, I–II, q. 90, a. 4.

[20] For the antecedent philosophical influences from Athens, Jerusalem, and Rome on the founding, and for the latter's connection to the Personalist/ Integrationist stream, see Robert L. Reilly, *America on Trial: A Defense of the Founding* (San Francisco: Ignatius Press, 2020).

Christian doctrine and natural law principles of the primacy of reason were thus indispensable elements in the development of American constitutionalism. Adherents to the PIA stream embraced these Christian principles as they started a movement that altered the face of America. As tempted as they were to succumb to pessimism altogether, they remained aligned with the stream built on hope and optimism. Martin Luther King's life serves as an icon of such commitment. In the face of constant criticism, he stood on the principles of the founders, even though some might question why. In his final "I've Been to the Mountain Top" speech, in which he sees himself in the shoes of Moses (Num. 27:12; Deut. 34), King said, "He's allowed me to go up to the mountain and I've looked over. And I've seen the Promised Land. I may not get there with you. But I want you to know tonight, that we, as a people, will get to the promised land!"[21] He was killed by an assassin's bullet the very next day.

THE DIALECTICAL NARRATIVE

The second understanding of race relations is the Dialectical/Separationist Approach (DSA). The dialectical approach sees human universalism as an aspiration instead of a point of departure. Universalism is obscured by oppression; thus, talk of universalism tends to ignore questions of justice. The DSA stream follows the vision of freedom affirmed by the non-Western mind, where freedom is realized only by full integration within the kin group and by the individual's conformity to the will and ultimate goals of the group. Each person is a drop within the great wave of ethnic belonging and, if faithful to the collective, that drop gains meaning. The point of departure is not the individual person, unique and unrepeatable, standing *sui generis*, but the group. Individual freedom is sacrificed at the altar of what Patterson calls "sovereignal freedom." Sovereignal freedom relieves the individual from isolation in exchange for loyal service, deference, and loyalty to the group. It is within the group that freedom is found, collectivized for the sake of survival. Conformity to the role, expectations, and culture of the group offers a necessary safety that prevents alienation into the nothingness of individuality.

---

[21] See the full text at American Rhetoric, https://www.americanrhetoric.com/speeches/mlkivebeentothemountaintop.htm.

The pull of such a conception is powerful because in the context of slavery, commonality as a method was crucial for survival in the face of brutality. It is also alluring because it is deterministic. If "the system" is the culprit for the lack of personal autonomy, there is a good reason to affirm that condition as part of one's identity. If being an individual Black person is a persistent woe informed by pitiless despair, and there is no expectation of reward for one's accomplishments, a collectivist explanation arrives almost by necessity. A given racial group is guilty (and their society instrumentally at fault) and another racial group is a haven of security, affirmation, contingency, and counterattack. In the face of self-doubt manufactured by the oppressor, groupthink seems a good place to relieve one's vulnerability, just as the non-Western tribal member saw in the kin group the practical solution to the perennial threat of enslavement and social death.[22] In this view, individual freedom as the matrix for understanding Black aspirations is an impediment to finding solutions, as it is as practically impossible today as it was practically impossible for tribesmen in the prehistoric savannas of Africa.

There is a real tension here as two civilizations and modes of understanding—the enslaver's and the enslaved—merged in the context of antagonism. Leading leftist scholars such as Derrick Bell reflect a dialectic of antagonism as they tell us the founding itself was the problem, as the founders betrayed the ideals to which they gave lip service.[23] The

---

[22] See Shelby Steele, *The Content of Our Character: A New Vision of Race in America* (New York: Harper Collins, 1990), chap. 3; Orlando Patterson, *The Ordeal of Integration* (New York: Basic Civitas, 1997), 86–92.

[23] "Racism is an integral, permanent, and indestructible component of this society." Derrick Bell, *Faces at the Bottom of the Well* (New York: New York University Press, 1992), ix. "I wonder how [freedom] feels? I am trapped and can only say 'Nooo' and hope my scream is loud enough to discourage the monsters and keep them back until I am strong enough, powerful enough to fight my way free." Ralph Wiley, *What Black People Should Do Now* (New York: Ballantine Books, 1993), 164. "Black Lives Matter is an ideological and political intervention in a world where Black lives are systematically and intentionally targeted for demise. It is an affirmation of Black folks' humanity, our contributions to this society, and our resilience in the face of deadly oppression." "Herstory," Black Lives Matter, accessed December 9, 2020, https://Blacklivesmatter.com/herstory/.

normal science[24] of this stream of thought has become the assertion that there were no values to adhere to that could serve as the link between those brought here in chains and the hope for eventual integration. In this view, an oppositional stance is the only way to affirm authentic love for the group, and Blacks at best could only aspire to become the "enemy within" American society. Just as slaves did among non-Western tribes such as the Tupimamba of the Amazon, Blacks might find a temporary place within the foreigners' group, but their destiny was social and physical death and their daily experience a combination of fear and contempt.[25] As Patterson explains, "Commitment to the autonomy and strength of the group often entails a submission of one's identity to that of the group. Collective freedom, collective power, and collective responsibility are all bought at the expense of the individual's complete suspension of, or submission to, the will of the group and its leaders."[26]

Malcolm X is probably the best-known exemplar of the separationist and dialectical stream of thought, which sees the Black American experience as a "nightmare"[27] and finds inspirational antecedents in the slave rebellion spearheaded by Nathanial "Nat" Turner (1800–1831) and the Black nationalism and Pan-Africanism of Marcus Garvey and the Nation of Islam. In the 1960s Stokely Carmichael and Willie Ricks popularized the "Black Power" slogan. Both were active in the Black Power movement as it became the sociopolitical arm of the dialectical stream, which served as a counterbalance to the personalist stream

---

[24] Thomas S. Kuhn, *The Structure of Scientific Revolutions*, 2nd ed. (Chicago: University of Chicago Press, [1962] 1970), 5. "Normal Science, the activity in which most scientists inevitably spend almost all their time, is predicated on the assumption that the scientific community knows what the world is like. Much of the success of the enterprise derives from the community's willingness to defend that assumption, if necessary, at considerable cost." A similar reality obtains in Black America's pull for commonality and political sameness and the often searing attacks on anyone who defies the racial normal science.

[25] Patterson, *Freedom in the Making*, 13–16.

[26] Patterson, *Ordeal of Integration*, 101.

[27] James H. Cone, *Martin & Malcolm & America: A Dream or a Nightmare* (New York: Orbis Books, 1991), 89; Alex Haley, *The Autobiography of Malcolm X* (New York: Ballantine Books, 1964), chap. 1.

by the latter part of the 1960s civil rights movement. Following the 1965 Watts riots in Los Angeles, the Student Nonviolent Coordinating Committee severed ties with the mainstream civil rights movement. This separation was an early hint of the ultimate clash between the Personalist and Dialectical streams. The more radical civil rights movement militants argued for the need to build power through forceful militancy that will allow for an eventual separation, instead of seeking integration through accommodation within the system called America. In a similar vein and during the same period, Bobby Seale founded the Black Panther Party.[28]

As this stream's narrative goes, America is a criminal enterprise that has forced Blacks into poverty, drug addiction, degradation, and crime, and only a dialectical severance from the essence of America, whether by radical alteration of its structures or actual physical (geographical) separation, will permit sovereignal freedom to be attained. The key to Western success and the essence of the American founding are not freedom but oppression: specifically, the crimes of ethnocentrism, colonialism, imperialism, and racism. And the key to ending this oppressive and irreformable system is power.

This understanding of race relations emphasizes collective identity, collective innocence, collective guilt, and collective and separate destiny. Race and the kin group become a basic reality, a sort of practical absolute, the heart of identity (racialist essentialism). Remarkably, we might add, the way this system reads American history is exactly the same way the infamous Chief Justice Roger Taney of the *Dread Scott* case and the rabid racists read history. The ground of understanding of the dialectical system is akin to the non-Western view of freedom and fully aligns with Marxist dialectical materialism and Marxist analysis of history.

Instead of class moving history forward, race is the catalyst. A racial "brotherhood" and the concept of *self-determination* acquire a similar meaning to that of Marxist *class consciousness*,[29] where the self is the

---

[28] See Editors of Encyclopedia Britannica, "Student Nonviolent Coordinating Committee," Encyclopedia Britannica, July 23, 2020, https://www.britannica.com/topic/Student-Nonviolent-Coordinating-Committee.

[29] Although Marx did not directly articulate a theory of class consciousness, he indirectly referred to it when characterizing the interests of the working class vis-à-vis the oppressive bourgeois class, which fostered an awareness of

racial group. For Marx, class consciousness is a phenomenon born out of historical collective struggle, which brings to bear objective features that must be shared by members of the group. Similarly, racial self-determination in this stream refers not to the fate of individuals who share an ancestry but the collective fate of those who share an ideology. The antithesis of class consciousness is *false consciousness*, and that false consciousness, when applied to the racial group, refers to individual members of the kin group who deviate from what is generally understood as the interests of the group vis-à-vis its oppressor. Again, individual freedom and integration become the enemies of the separatist and dialectical stream. Collective self-determination is not seen instrumentally as the context within which individual responsibility is appropriated and individual freedom enhanced; instead, the ultimate goal is fusion of the self with group consciousness.[30]

As collective identity is the mark for both the oppressor and the oppressed, only antagonism lies ahead. Integration deprives the racial victim of his identity, diluting it as a way of eliminating it. The dialectical stream is often accepted by people who seem in some respects successfully integrated, but it is never a final destination, only a step in the quest for power. The final goal remains complete separation at one end (Nation of Islam) and complete transformation of society at the other (most Black radical groups).

This dialectical understanding is engulfing us and has become the mainstream narrative in academia, politics, the media, and even many religious groups. It informs the claims of the 1619 Project. The radical difference between the two streams of thought reflects the ancient tension between the primacy of reason and that of the will. It is the tension between optimism built on the engines of reason and faith, which is aligned with the Western development of the idea of individual freedom, on one hand; and on the other, pessimism and the collectivist pursuit of power, which is aligned with the non-Western

the proletariat as a social class. It is in the thought of the French historian Jules Michelet that we might find an antecedent to the idea that social classes with distinctive features displace each other from power. In his 1867 *Histoire de France*, Michelet argues that one of the most salient features of the French Revolution was the displacement in power of one social class, the nobility, in favor of another, the bourgeoisie.

[30] For a good discussion see Patterson, *Ordeal of Integration*, 99–102.

understanding of sovereignal freedom. Ultimately intertwined as they are with such perennial questions, these two streams are also implicated in the great ideological battles of our generation, conflicts between individual freedom as understood in the West and in free market economies, and Marxist-Leninist collectivism and its many manifestations, revisions, and united fronts.

From the beginning of the civil rights movement, these warring camps were in evidence. The collectivist stream eventually captured the high ground with its appeal to the will, to raw emotion, to the most basic instincts of fallen man, and to ideologies that shared the ancient non-Western emphasis on avoiding social death by clinging to the group. Race became the necessary epiphenomenon of class and as such, it was only race that could save us.[31]

---

[31] Ironically, the instrumental weapon of the moment had its roots in old Europe, in the thought of Rousseau, Feuerbach, Hegel, and Marx.

3

DIVERSITIES, TRUE AND FALSE*

Ismael Hernandez
and
Kevin Schmiesing

O f the many abused terms in our day, *diversity* is a prominent one. In many parts of American society, it has become the holy grail, the achievement to be pursued above all others. Educational, economic, and cultural success either take lower priority or are in fact measured by it.

All of which raises the question: What is it?

RACE ABOVE ALL

Within the diversity industry, the term seems to mean preeminently racial or ethnic distinction. Leaving aside the enormous problem of racial definition, this is a highly restrictive view of diversity—yet it dominates the arena as though it is self-evidently the most important kind of human difference to recognize.

The arguments for promoting this form of diversity normally run along two tracks. One is the claim that diversity enhances the performance, authenticity, or excellence of the organization in question by

* Portions of this chapter were previously published at the Freedom and Virtue Foundation website, https://www.fvinstitute.org/newspress/, and as chapter 2 in Ismael Hernandez, *Not Tragically Colored: Freedom, Personhood, and the Renewal of Black America* (Grand Rapids: Acton Institute, 2016).

bringing a variety of voices and perspectives to the table. The other is that there is an obligation in justice to provide opportunity for members of all groups.

Both of these rationales are generally defensible at the level of principle. The management of institutions is improved by taking into account a number of perspectives. People should have the opportunity to advance and succeed regardless of their background or personal characteristics (assuming that those characteristics do not inherently disqualify them from the activity in question).

Yet the acceptance of these ideas in principle leaves open expansive areas of debate as to how they are to be applied in practice. In many circles, it seems to be accepted as axiomatic that race is the chief marker of diversity. Why should this be so?

Arguments in favor of using race as the primary gauge of diversity can be answered by counterexamples. Race should be the criterion, one argument goes, because Black Americans have been systematically discriminated against and are therefore underrepresented. Yet, it is a well-documented fact that political conservatives have been discriminated against systematically in the nation's most prestigious universities and that their numbers are consequently vanishingly small at those places. In many departments, (racial) minority faculty outnumber conservative faculty. Yet concerted efforts to recruit minorities continue, while there is no admission that the lack of conservatives is even a problem.

Religious identity is another neglected category. In 2020, California passed a bill requiring companies' boards of directors to diversify. One lawmaker advocating for the measure argued that it would ensure that "all of California's corporate boards will better reflect the diversity of our state."[1] But the bill, like almost every such program, focuses only on a particular species of diversity. California's corporate boards will contain more Blacks and Hispanics, but does that mean that they will *ipso facto* "better reflect the diversity" of the state? They will do so only if it is conceded that racial diversity alone is the kind of diversity that matters. Will the boards better reflect the religious diversity of the state? Will the number of board members of each company match

---

[1] K. Lloyd Billingsley, "California Imposes Diversity Dogma on Corporate Boards," Independent Institute, October 12, 2020, https://www.independent.org/news/article.asp?id=13293.

the percentages of Californians who identify as evangelical Christian, Muslim, Jewish, Catholic, Mormon, or atheist? Again, if the rationale for diversity promotion is rectification of past wrongs, all of these religious groups qualify. Each has been discriminated against, sometimes viciously so, at one time or another over the course of American history. On that ground, we should be sensitive to their representation in the higher echelons of society. Religious belief is an extraordinarily powerful source of meaning and shaper of worldview. Therefore, if we are looking for diversity of opinion, surely religion ought to be taken into account.

Innumerable other sources of diversity could be adduced: profession, temperament, interest, economic class, education, geography, and so on. All of them are important, yet virtually none of them ever matters when generating diversity metrics. As a result, in many sectors of American life, in the midst of unprecedented institutional commitment to diversity, there is ironically *decreasing* diversity. Obsession with "White" and "Black" and "Hispanic" to the exclusion of other criteria has resulted in growing geographical and vocational homogeneity along lines of income, education, and ideology.[2]

A SHALLOW SEA OF COLOR

Besides the arbitrary nature of using race as the primary marker of diversity, there is a deeper problem: the dehumanization of the "beneficiaries" of diversity crusades. In the minds of many, diversity is similar to taking a stroll at the local zoo to observe various species of animals or sitting comfortably at home to enjoy your aquarium. This taxonomical understanding of diversity is impoverished and tenuous. It leads to loss of respect for the person as we drown in an expansive yet shallow sea of color.

A personal anecdote will illustrate the problem. Ismael is a Black Puerto Rican and his wife is African American. In contemporary diversity terms, they check the boxes. Some years ago, their daughter

---

[2] For various aspects of this development, see, *inter alia*, Bill Bishop, with Robert G. Cushing, *The Big Sort: Why the Clustering of Like-Minded Americans Is Tearing Us Apart* (Boston: Houghton Mifflin, 2008); and Charles A. Murray, *Coming Apart: The State of White America, 1960–2010* (New York: Crown Forum, 2012).

graduated from high school with an impressive academic resume. It was exciting for her to start applying for college, and one of her top choices sent her an invitation to a "scholars' night." She was excited about the opportunity.

Ismael's wife joined their daughter for a weekend at the university. The initial event was an evening reception, and as they entered a large room, they noticed dozens of students already there. As the evening proceeded, more students joined, but the daughter noticed something curious: only Black and brown students were present. She exclaimed to her mother, "There are no White scholars at this university!"

They soon discovered that most students there had extremely low grade-point averages. The "scholars' night" was no such thing; it was merely a ploy by diversity bureaucrats to meet their quota of students of color. In other words, they did not see Ismael's daughter as an individual who had worked hard and excelled and was seeking an educational path to realize her full potential. Instead, they saw her skin color. Mother and daughter packed and left the university immediately—after expressing to organizers their disappointment at the disrespect and "soft bigotry of low expectations."[3]

Although such efforts are often couched in the rhetoric of justice for a deprived people and rationalized as a desire to prop up those whose starting line was far behind, they only achieve the severing of the connection between reward and accomplishment—the connection that permits the attainment of genuine success by overcoming obstacles through discipline and struggle. Offering bonus points to "endangered communities," however well-intentioned, is a species of degrading and condescending paternalism.

As Chief Justice John Roberts put it in a 2007 decision, "The way to stop discrimination on the basis of race is to stop discriminating on the basis of race."[4] Yet the diversity industry foments race-consciousness, seemingly oblivious to the ways in which this perpetuates the race-reductionism that the civil rights movement aimed to destroy. A

---

[3] The phrase was coined by President George W. Bush in a speech to the 91st convention of the NAACP. George W. Bush's Speech to the NAACP, July 10, 2000, https://www.washingtonpost.com/wp-srv/onpolitics/elections/bushtext071000.htm.

[4] *Parents Involved in Community Schools v. Seattle School Dist. No. 1,* 551 US 701 (2007), https://supreme.justia.com/cases/federal/us/551/701/.

prime example was the distasteful race-and-ethnicity-laden quarrel over the spoils of presidential appointments in the early days of the Biden administration, which saw senators quibbling about how many posts should go to Asian Americans and who counted as such. Jim Geraghty of *National Review* correctly observed, "Instead of judging those nominees by their merits, those senators *pledged to judge them by the color of their skin.*" He concluded sardonically, "If only we had a word to describe that phenomenon."[5]

The fact remains that we are not as different from each other as the diversity industry promulgates. There is no profound cultural divide in America that is not the product of the constant drumbeat that there is one. To be sure, there are differences in customs, accents, and ways of doing things, but they are only balkanizing if we accept the progressive ideology behind the allegations of radical differences—an ideology that is not part of the culture of those deemed to be in cultural diaspora and must be imposed to convince them of the deplorable state of affairs.

The diversity-centric worldview strives to replace the traditional "melting pot" metaphor with an ideologically driven "salad bowl": we are no longer a unified culture formed from the melding of many disparate cultures but instead a heterogeneous mix of separate identities.[6] As America was an experiment in ideas, diversity activists want to impose a new set of ideas to convince minorities that their land is far away, in a foreign Valhalla. They reject America as a common enterprise of common values. By asserting that there are fundamental differences at play, they can convince us that diversity necessitates a complete rearrangement of the body politic. The insistence on skin-deep diversity—that is, race—gives the diversity party a way to highlight some differences and ignore many commonalities, in the process filling the agnostic space they have cleared in our minds with gnostic knowledge of some imaginary "real" Blackness or Hispanicness. If cultural features exist merely as badges of honor to create barriers for

---

[5] Jim Geraghty, "Senate Democrats' Short-Lived Opposition to All White Biden Nominees," *National Review,* March 24, 2021, https://www.national-review.com/the-morning-jolt/senate-democrats-short-lived-opposition-to-all-White-biden-nominees.

[6] Peter Wood, *Diversity: The Invention of a Concept* (San Francisco: Encounter Books, 2003), 22–28.

unity, the creation of a diverse community is an impossibility. Culture becomes a weapon and diversity becomes an empty word.

Inclusive Monoculturalism

Inclusive monoculturalism is a better description of the set of ideas under which an overlapping social consensus may be feasible. The concept embraces a variety of cultural expressions and even compatible comprehensive views within the framework of American political, social, and economic institutions, while retaining the foundational features of our Western civilization heritage. Inclusive monoculturalism is not neutral with respect to culture but affirms the primacy of Western civilization in the formation of our sociopolitical ecology. As individuals from other cultures enter the mainstream of American life, some of their cultural mores may find a place in our midst *if* they are compatible with the American principles of human dignity, rule of law, constitutionalism, democracy, tolerance, and the basic ethical tenets of the Christian faith.[7]

This embrace of other cultures, however, cannot be absolute. Only those aspects of cultures (and of their corresponding comprehensive views) compatible with traditional mores based on our Western cultural heritage are to be accepted as consistent with what philosopher Robert P. George calls a "reasonable moral agreement ... on fair terms of cooperation" among citizens.[8] In other words, only contributions true to type are to be embraced and included in the creation of an American culture that continues to adapt without losing its essential features. American culture is seen in a *foundational* rather than in an *essentialist* fashion. This means that American culture is not viewed as unalterable but as providing a set of cherished basic beliefs.

Inclusive monoculturalism recognizes the need for what Joseph Raz labels "social forms," offering recognition to certain values affirmed through the polity's formal institutions. Public affirmation of a uni-

---

[7] By basic ethical tenets we mean basic understandings of the human person captured in documents such as the Declaration of Independence— which was mostly successful in reflecting an anthropology consistent with Christian natural law.

[8] Robert P. George, *In Defense of Natural Law* (New York: Oxford University Press, 2001), 200.

fying cultural commonality provides a framework of expectations and affirms society's commitment to certain values. Making a social commitment to a given culture provides a boundary within which the value of autonomy is affirmed. That commitment will shape people's cultural options and offer intelligibility to the country's cultural life. As these cultural commitments are social choices, autonomy is not suppressed by providing a boundary.[9]

There is, however, a *private* moral pluralism that affirms the existence of diverse valuable forms of life. One can affirm the goodness of certain private cultural expressions and the possibility of eventually incorporating them (or not) into the general culture without having to accept *every* cultural expression. This is not akin to relativism, as it recognizes that there may be unworthy cultural expressions.[10]

Individuals in their private affairs are free to practice other particular cultural expressions. They are also responsible for their preservation, as the state neither discourages them nor presses for their inclusion. As individuals live their lives in free association with others, certain new expressions will become part of our heritage without any attempt by the state to direct these impulses. Other compatible expressions will endure among those who continue to value them. without necessarily expanding their sphere of recognition. No ethnic group or race is enthroned over others.

DIVERSITY IS NOT VICTIMHOOD

About 14 percent of Americans are of Hispanic descent. That is a fact. The fact shows a difference. But is that difference necessarily divisive? No. It becomes problematic when it is used as a tool, as a weapon to mince society into discrete groups with "proportional representation" everywhere. What is merely a beautiful expression of uniqueness within a society informed by inclusive monocultural features based on a common set of principles, is transformed into a radically divisive tool for power. Groups are competing for the same resources and one

[9] Joseph Raz, *The Morality of Freedom* (Oxford, UK: Clarendon Press, 1986), 164–67.

[10] On the idea of pluralistic perfectionism and autonomy see Robert P. George, *Making Men Moral: Civil Liberties and Public Morality* (Oxford, UK: Clarendon Press, 1993), 162–73.

group is dominant over the others, making the struggle a dialectical one. This ghettoization of the entire body politic of necessity leads to separatism as the only solution.

Rearranging the whole society for the victims is offered to Whites as their way of redemption for a past that is continually placed in front of them. That past is a ticket to redemption for them and a Pyrric victory for minorities. Minorities become "endangered," "different," "special," because the status of victims confers benefit at the expense of being seen in the full scope of their personhood. The demands made on Whites are impossible, while the ones placed on minorities are minimal. How else, for example, can we understand the attention given to cases of homicide by police in comparison to the virtual indifference toward the avalanche of internal community violence sweeping the inner city? If we can place internal community problems always in the context of the effects of systemic victimization, there is not much to do but become political activists.

This is all an ideological ploy based on the dialectics of history that must find culprits and victims, oppressors and oppressed, expropriated and expropriators. In reality, diversity would be unsettling to Marxists because when we, for example, study ancient cultures around the world, we find that they tend (with some exceptions) to be patriarchal and very traditional in mores and cultural and sexual ethics. This is one reason why liberation theologies developed in old Europe and are based on the thought of an elderly, anti-Semitic Prussian! The young seminarians at Tübingen and Rome concocted a theory that was in many ways at odds with the culture of the people they claimed to represent. With focused zeal, they descended into the barrios and favelas of Central and South America to snatch the culture and paint it with a veneer of ideology. After their indoctrination was all but complete, they suddenly claimed that the now-ideologized version of culture they imposed had to be respected by the colonial powers.

Diversity, it should be clear, is not a single thing nor a simple thing. It is inextricably tied to human identity, which is a complex phenomenon that is expressed in complex ways. As an expression of genetic and cultural variety, it is a fact of existence, and comprehension of human experience requires its acknowledgment and appreciation. But *diversity* employed bluntly, as though it is reducible to one dimension of identity (e.g., race) and as though it automatically implies certain policies (e.g., affirmative action) becomes nothing more than a rhetorical weapon in the arsenal of the demagogue. Yet more problematically, this debasement of the concept permits its enlistment in the cause of Marxist ideology, as yet another category of oppression and source of ineluctable societal conflict. We must reject these false diversities and return to the true diversity of the founding era, which sought what was common among a pluralistic people. *E pluribus unum*: From many, one.

4

Genuine Social Justice*

Ismael Hernandez

We hear much about justice these days, but the concept is seldom defined by those crying for it. As theoretician Anthony de Jasay tells us in his great book *Justice and Its Surroundings*, "It is one of the most pervasive fallacies of contemporary political theory, that, one way or another, normatively if not positively, every unfulfilled need, every blow of ill luck, every disparity of endowments, every case of conspicuous success or failure, and every curtailment of liberties, is a question of justice."[1]

If that were the case, every social interaction would be a question of justice, with justice erasing every other virtue. It would make justice unintelligible and its attainment a matter of mere subjective desire or appetite or of the power available to impose a given answer. This is the dominant approach among contemporary race activists, for whom justice has become an all-encompassing rhetorical tool used to promote whatever political or social aim being pursued. This corruption of the ideal of justice has been abetted by the rise of the derivative term *social justice*.

---

* Portions of this chapter were previously published at the Freedom and Virtue Institute website, https://www.fvinstitute.org/newspress/.

[1] Anthony de Jasay, *Justice and Its Surroundings* (Indianapolis: Liberty Fund, 2002).

Justice lies at the heart of legitimate government and therefore it is too important to abandon. Instead, we must prune away the accretions that have distorted its meaning, return to the classic view, and clearly define its varieties, such as social justice.

Justice in Action

To correct a perceived wrong in the distant past is not a matter of justice. Some think that society today must correct every wrong committed during slavery and that the descendants of slaves today are owed such recompense, in justice. The thought, as lofty as its proponents might deem it, has nothing to do with justice. States of affairs are not strictly speaking just or unjust; they simply *are*. Actions—specific actions—might be unjust.

A state of affairs might deviate from an ideal, and we might find that historically there was a fault in the alignment of just action and a said state of affairs. We can, in that context, speak of an injustice. However, in the here and now, we can only tie justice to personal responsibility and to a set of rules that are in themselves just or unjust by being equal or unequal in the areas pertinent to equal treatment. A "system" is not at fault the same way persons are at fault in their individual acts. A system might be at fault not if it fails to accomplish the impossible—that is, erasing the errors of the long-gone past—but if it still possesses formal rules that perpetuate the injustice.

If formal rules failing in equal treatment in areas relevant to the exercise of rights are no longer in place, we have accomplished justice. The fact that various actors get to that line at variant social states is insignificant to justice.

Attempts to find justice where there is no personal responsibility for a given act are often exercises in hubris or in ideology. They are hubris because we do not possess the comprehensive insight into reality that is required to piece together existence and determine with certainty what could have happened in history absent an event as it was. Nor can we trace responsibility for evil actions throughout the centuries so as to locate a culprit in the present.

They are ideology when one believes that a collective class of people rather than the individual is the determinant of history, and that every member of a class is a specimen of that class and thereby innocent or guilty, deserving redress or punishment. Indictment is categorical, and the solution is dependent on the power to impose a solution. But that is not justice properly understood, whereby every individual person, as a moral agent of choice, acts, and his acts bring about a molding of character and accountability for choices taken.

In short, justice is not about relieving feelings of unease about a past for which one bears no responsibility, even if, as some claim, one's present state is better as a consequence.

THE DEMANDS OF JUSTICE

The loss of the traditional understanding of justice has opened the door to confusing ideas regarding the demands of justice. In its most basic sense, justice pertains to what is owed to another and is satisfied when the one owed receives what is his, *suum cuique.* Justice is a virtue, inasmuch as the trait exists in an individual person, who exhibits the habit of giving to each his due. When referring to the virtue in persons, we call it commutative justice. Justice primarily exists in individual persons, but it can be also expressed in the law of a community when, aligned with right reason, the law becomes a guarantor of that exercise of giving to each his own. When justice pertains to the relationship of an individual to a community—community being a group of persons united for a common purpose—it is called distributive justice. In the latter, there are two sets of obligations; namely, obligations of individuals toward the community and of the community toward individuals.

Our first duty as we confront the troubling times we are experiencing today is to make a firm resolve to render to each his due. To place our hearts at the service of justice is to place our whole being at its service. To know what is just, however, we must first know what is good. Both the objective norms of morality coming from special revelation and those flowing from the natural law assist us in discovering what is good for man qua man and for man in community. There are both objective absolute or exceptionless norms as well as prudential norms that must govern interactions between two people, a person and society, and society as a whole.

Sincerity and civil law are not enough. A man who is in the habit of conforming to the moral law and the natural law is better prepared when prudence calls for making decisions where there exist alternative courses of action. A person who, ignoring these norms, appeals to a secular political program, will certainly fail, despite claims of acting justly. The temptation to seek justice by any means, even by inflicting unjust treatment on others if necessary, is always there, as the base inclinations of our appetites incline us all to get what we demand on any terms of our liking.

Justice is a habit, but so is tyranny. As Dostoevsky said, "Tyranny is a habit; it may develop and it does develop, at last, into a disease. I maintain that the very best of men may be coarsened and hardened into a brute by habit."[2] He was referring to Marxism. Ideologies can talk about justice when they really mean power or revenge, embodied in a narrative of history and of action that justifies evil and brutalizes our conscience.

That is why we must resist the temptation to see justice as an ideology. An ideology is a system of ideas that stimulates action. The most mobilizing ideologies indeed speak about justice and narrowly construe its parameters, depriving it of its meaning as a habit and making it a postulate within a narrative. The most successful ideologies are about the triumph of the will, not about the cultivation of virtue. They stimulate the mouth to shouting, turn protests into mobs, use images as weapons, and often bathe the streets in blood—all in the name of justice.

These ideologies use injustice even gleefully to channel pain to an ideological target. In the process, as it was with fascism, it speaks of lofty goals such as unity, humanity, peace, love, harmony, dignity, and, yes, justice—social justice. The ultimate aim, however, is the destruction of the other.

Ideology has an advantage over other constructs: it gives you a simple plan, a clear target, an assured comfort that we have identified the error and we can now extirpate it. But there are consequences, powerful social consequences. Authentic social justice is not *social* because it is political or pertains to governmental policy or initiative. It is social because it inclines the person toward the common good. The free and responsible actions of those who have made space in their souls for justice are what we call "social justice."

---

[2] Fyodor Dostoevsky, *The House of the Dead: A Novel in Two Parts*, trans. Constance Garnett (New York: Macmillan, 1915), 186.

SOCIAL JUSTICE

Modern theology calls distributive justice *social justice*. It is rather unfortunate, because the traditional rendering avoids the merger of social justice with political platforms and political ideologies. People hear *social justice* and they think they hear *socialism*—with either positive or negative connotations, depending on the listener's perspective.

The social justice that we ought to pursue is not the social justice of the socialist ideology or the partisan plan of a radicalized group. Claims of pursuing justice can at times become an excuse for anger, retribution, control, or the disregard of moral norms. That is why the radical sees justice as the ultimate end and prudence as cowardice. Justice must be tempered and supplemented with such virtues as empathy, prudence, solidarity, love, mercy, and forgiveness. This is why Michael Novak argues that social justice is "a habit of the heart embodied in individual persons" that inaugurates "a set of new habits and abilities that need to be learned, perfected, and passed on to new generations—new virtues with very powerful social consequences."[3]

For most people, social justice refers to the distribution of benefits in society. The original meaning of social justice, however, had nothing to do with the distribution of anything. The popular understanding of social justice is captured by the *American Sociological Review*:

> As I see it, social justice requires resource equity, fairness, and respect for diversity, as well as the eradication of existing forms of social oppression. Social justice entails a redistribution of resources from those who have unjustly gained them to those who justly deserve them, and it also means creating and ensuring the processes of truly democratic participation in decision-making.... It seems clear that only a decisive redistribution of resources and decision-making power can ensure social justice and authentic democracy.[4]

---

[3] Michael Novak and Paul Adams, with Elizabeth Shaw, *Social Justice Isn't What You Think It Is* (New York: Encounter, 2015), 22–23.

[4] Joe R. Feagin, "Social Justice and Sociology: Agendas for the Twenty-First Century: Presidential Address," *American Sociological Review* 66, no. 1 (February 2001): 5, https://www.jstor.org/stable/2657391.

Arithmetical uniformity is at the heart of this new definition. It is full of indictments with an "us against them" flavor. More importantly, it requires an agent in charge of enforcing the said rearrangement of benefits. That entity is none other than the state. This definition of social justice is statist by providing to central bodies the power to confiscate and to determine what is just. This is really a dreadful change in the meaning of social justice, because to accomplish it you must give an enormous amount of power to the equalizer: the state.

The concept of redistribution implies that benefits are not earned in the first place, so the success of some is illegitimate and in need of correction. That concept is also collectivist, as redress is owed to people as groups. Certain characteristics provide members of groups the right to receive benefits and certain characteristics demand that members of other groups contribute something. Who is supposed to balance things? The state. Alongside the notion of collective redress are the notions of collective victimization and collective guilt. The implications of such an understanding of how society works are severe for the prospect of social cohesion. At the end of that path is not justice but mutual resentment, because the appetite for victimization is insatiable and guilt becomes a stigma.

More importantly, the modern mind has become so ingrained with the alluring music of social justice that the mere mention of it weakens the resolve to resist what otherwise might be seen as nonsense. As Friedrich Hayek surmised, "The appeal to 'social justice' has nevertheless by now become the most widely used and most effective argument in political discussion. Almost every claim for government action on behalf of particular groups is advanced by its name, and if it can be made to appear that a certain measure is required by 'social justice,' opposition to it will rapidly weaken."[5]

---

[5] Friedrich Hayek, *The Mirage of Social Justice*, vol. 2 of *Law, Legislation & Liberty* (Chicago: University of Chicago Press, 1976), 65.

THE COMMON GOOD AND COMPASSION

A term often employed in tandem with social justice is the *common good*. A wonderful term in itself, its meaning in practice often hinges on a key question; namely, *who decides* what is the common good. In contemporary times that responsibility gradually shifted to the bureaucratic state. The beautiful notion of the common good thereby got ensnared in red tape and battles for power. The common good has become an excuse for state control, the passing of laws, the expansion of the bureaucratic state, and government decision-making—so much so that most people think immediately of the government and "what are they going to do" every time there is a crisis.

As the state has become the agent of social justice, people can eschew personal responsibility and fix their gaze on impersonal structures. Structures now have become a living being, a system that can be blamed or praised according to a collectivist ideology. Interestingly, the common good has often been the excuse on which totalitarianism has been built. You can achieve the common good better if there is a total authority, one that limits the desires and actions of individuals. Individual aims are seen as problematic and divisive, and any system purporting to defend individual rights, such as the right to property or even the right to have your own opinion, must be challenged. Political correctness, statism, and collectivism are all engendered by a false notion of social justice.

Closely associated with social justice and the common good is the word *compassion*. In modern times, an extraordinary number of bad things have been done in the name of compassion for the poor. Modern revolutions are almost all fought in the name of the poor and the oppressed. More sins have been committed in the name of compassion in the last 150 years than by any other force in history.

We must not allow that beautiful term to blind us. The word is so powerful that people forget what instrument is being used to effect a result. "By all means necessary" seems about right, as long as the claim is that we are being compassionate. In a strict sense, compassion means to be there with the one who suffers—it is an individual call to action and solidarity that may or may not alleviate the problem but is always faithfully present and involved in the act of suffering. But again, if social justice is about group entitlement and centralized action, individual responsibility to suffer with the other is madness!

Authentic Social Justice

Bertrand de Jouvenel is correct in stating that "it is a loose modern habit to call 'just' whatever is thought emotionally desirable."[6] The dictatorship of appetite can camouflage as social justice. It is easy to feel that whatever we see as in need of change necessitates an intervention. The proportional distribution of resources according to need is just around the corner of an emotional appeal to fix things. Just as it feels improper that some lack what they need, it feels wrong that in our estimation some have more than they need. Who is to restore the proper balance? The state. Upon a society rebelling against its capacity to raise the standard of living to unimaginable highs soon falls a weight of guilt that triggers the eager hands of the statists. All of this shuffling of earned resources to unearning hands has been called social justice.

The loss of the traditional understanding of social justice has resulted in confusion and abandonment of the term by many. It is primarily a virtue of individuals. I must develop the sense that I ought to give to others what they deserve. A person is just when that person develops the habit of giving to others (either other individuals or a community) what is owed to them. Social justice directs the acts of individuals toward the common good. In the end, social justice is a virtue of individuals or it is a fraud.[7]

Alexis de Tocqueville said the most fascinating and insightful thing about America that relates to the authentic sphere of social justice. In the United States, he observed, people get together and form associations. They hold bake sales to send missionaries to the Antipodes and to build colleges. They invent hundreds of devices to raise money among themselves. That is what a free people do. The Americans of Tocqueville's time took personal responsibility for the common good as each saw an individual duty to give something to their community. That is social justice: not what the community owes to groups by way of state power but what individuals and free associations of individuals owe to each other and to their society.

---

[6] Bertrand de Jouvenel, *The Ethics of Redistribution* (Indianapolis: Liberty Fund, 1990), 18.

[7] Michael Novak, "Defining Social Justice," *First Things* (December 2000), https://www.firstthings.com/article/2000/12/defining-social-justice.

And that is what, in a word, social justice is: a virtue, a habit that people internalize and learn, a capacity. It is a capacity that has two elements: first, organizing with others to accomplish particular ends; and second, pursuing ends that are extrafamilial—that is, for the good of the neighborhood, the town, the state, or the world.

Finally, it is important to note that this correct notion of social justice is ideologically neutral. It is as common for people on the left to organize and form associations, to cooperate in social projects, as it is for people on the right. This is not a loaded political definition, but it does avoid the pitfall (on the left) of thinking that social justice means redistribution, *égalité,* the common good only as determined by state authority. It also avoids the pitfall (on the right) of thinking of the individual as unencumbered, self-contained, self-sufficient, and interested only in personal welfare.

5

CIVIL RIGHTS AND CIVIL UNREST*

Ismael Hernandez and Kevin Schmiesing

There are many fault lines running through American culture today: Black and White, Christian and atheist, liberal and conservative. But there is one that crosscuts these other divisions and that poses an existential threat to the future of the Republic. It is the line between barbarism and civilization.

For ancient Greeks and Romans, the *barbarian* was a foreigner: a German or Briton or African who did not share the culture of law, philosophy, technology, and religion that characterized the great Mediterranean empires. Gradually, however, the term came to apply less to ethnic or national boundaries and more to education and etiquette. Those who were trained in and accepted the dominant customs, manners, and mores of society could be considered "civilized"; those who rejected those norms in one way or another behaved "barbarically."

In our casual and egalitarian age, when behaviors such as coarse language and sloppy dress no longer disqualify one from respectable society, the very idea of distinguishing between civilized and barbarian strikes many as offensive. But the distinction ought to be rehabilitated

---

* Portions of this chapter were previously published at the Freedom and Virtue Institute website, https://www.fvinstitute.org/newspress/.

in the present climate, even if its meaning has shifted. For one of the marks of civilization is the gathering of people in cities (*civitas* in Latin), where they participate freely and peacefully in politics and commerce. This requires adherence to a rule of law regarding respect for property and persons.

Unfortunately, the widespread lack of such respect is increasingly evident. The summer of 2020 was awash in violence against persons and property, most notably in Seattle, where order was forthrightly abandoned and anarchy permitted to run amok.[1] This barbarism is not unique to the political left or the political right; it can be found wherever confrontation with difference erupts into shouting, shoving, or shooting. It can be found among politicians, police officers, and pastors, as well as activists, anarchists, and adolescents of all ages. As the Reverend Dean Nelson of the Frederick Douglass Foundation said in the wake of an incident in which a statue of Douglass was vandalized, "There are people within our culture that are more committed to creating chaos than they are solving problems and finding solutions."[2]

The widespread nature of these instances of mob rule and violence is one marker of the rise of barbarism. An even more distressing one is the unwillingness of broad swaths of the American elite to condemn them unequivocally. In some cities, mayors and other officials have given free rein to property destruction and even assault.

Without question, there are among us wide and deep differences of position and opinion on crucial matters of politics, economics, and morality. We do not agree on how to combat poverty or racism or disease. But in the midst of such diversity there are only two options: Working through differences in the context of fundamental agreement on the standards of conduct and debate and adjudicating them through fair and consistent political processes; or settling them

---

[1] See Jason Rantz, "I'm Reporting from Seattle's CHOP. Here's What It's Really Been Like," The Daily Signal, June 29, 2020, https://www.dailysignal.com/2020/06/29/im-reporting-from-seattles-chop-heres-what-its-really-been-like/.

[2] Interview with Virginia Allen, "Frederick Douglass Statue Toppling Is About 'Creating Chaos,'" The Daily Signal, July 7, 2020, https://www.dailysignal.com/2020/07/07/frederick-douglass-statue-toppling-is-about-creating-chaos/.

by force and violence according to the barbaric principle of "might makes right."

This is a deeply ironic moment. Most of the progress the world has made with respect to the treatment of ethnic and racial minorities, women, and other out-of-favor or out-of-power groups, has come about precisely because appeals to sound moral principles have triumphed over "might makes right." Those who, in the name of social justice, are fomenting a turn to violent settlement of disputes are playing a dangerous game, one that will ultimately result in *regress* in the quest for justice and equality.

Unless we can agree on the unexceptionable tenets of respect for other human beings and law and order, the common pursuit of other aims can never even start.

PEACE AND JUSTICE

One justification offered for the descent into violent protest is reflected in the expression "No Justice, No Peace." What does this slogan mean?

Admonitions on how to bring about peace in the world are not new. As early as 385 AD, the Roman military expert Vegetius in his influential military treatise wrote, "*Igitur qui desiderat pacem, praeparet bellum*" ("Therefore let him who desires peace prepare for war").[3] To this day we are preoccupied with justice and peace and how they interrelate. This is why we must ask whether the slogan "No Justice, No Peace" is reasonable.[4]

The slogan can be understood either as a *conditional* or a *conjunctive* statement. The conditional renders the proposition as an "if-then"

---

[3] Flavius Vegetius Renatus, *Epitoma Rei Militaris*, bk. 3. The Latin Library, http://www.thelatinlibrary.com/vegetius3.html.

[4] The origin of the slogan is unclear, but it seems to have gained popularity during the racial antagonism and protests in the mid-1980s. See Ben Zimmer, "No Justice, No Peace," Language Log, July 15, 2013, https://languagelog .ldc.upenn.edu/nll/?p=5249. Martin Luther King Jr. voiced a similar idea on several occasions: for example, in a letter to Willem Visser 't Hooft: "There can be no justice without peace. And there can be no peace without justice." Quoted in Thomas A. Mulhall, *A Lasting Prophetic Legacy: Martin Luther King Jr., The World Council of Churches, and the Global Crusade Against Racism and War* (Eugene, OR: Wipf & Stock, 2014), 51.

statement, meaning that in the absence of justice peace is not possible. Essentially, a condition of injustice leads to a condition of absence of peace even if war is not present. Injustice triggers alienation, and alienation can lead to disintegration because the right relations between men are disturbed. One can ascertain that it is reasonable to believe that if injustice exists, there is no real peace, and the conditions exist to bring about violence.

In the context of racial politics, however, it becomes more than a statement of fact and reasonable expectation, meaning that if there is no justice, we might not get peace. Instead, it is an invitation to the use of force, as peaceful protest is useless in acquiring justice. As a proposition, it invites people to see a problem within the dialectical understanding that only the use of force will move the "oppressor" to rescind his privileges. It tells people that the existing structures of society cannot possibly attend their quest, as the structures are inherently racist and thus unjust—so the theory of systemic racism explains. It is difficult to see how the conclusion that the social system of America is ultimately and inexorably destined for dissolution can fail to lead us to despair. The conditional renders the use of peaceful protest illusory and ineffective and calls for the framing of the struggle for justice in the right instrumental fashion. It is a call to arms, or better, a call to accept a very specific ideological system as a prerequisite to eventuate justice and peace.

By contrast, the slogan understood in the conjunctive form states that neither peace nor justice can exist without the other. The conjunctive provides a conclusion: the absence of justice has resulted in a lack of peace. Al Sharpton, for example, has written as much, "'No justice, no peace' … is a way to expose inequality that would otherwise be ignored."[5]

In other words, the phrase asserts a very specific understanding of an existing structural condition. We must understand that society is unjust and that the violence we see is the necessary result of injustice. As such, we may or may not agree with the assertion that the violence we see is the result of injustice. After all, violence can serve other

---

[5] Al Sharpton. "No Justice, No Peace: Why Mark Duggan's Family Echoed My Rallying Cry," *The Guardian,* January 10, 2014, https://www.theguardian.com/commentisfree/2014/jan/10/mark-duggan-family-rallying-cry-no-peace-no-justice.

purposes. Ideologies use violence, and people with personal or group gain in mind use violence.

For example, Martin Luther King Jr. understood the substance of the slogan in the conjunctive. The reality of structural racism, still alive and well during his time, motivated him and others to protest peacefully. However, they were met with violence; there was no peace. Notice that he did not accept the slogan in the conditional, at least not in the conditional as presented within a dialectical framework. He believed that peaceful protest had both instrumental and moral value, and violence, even in the presence of actual injustice, was not necessary. Powerfully, King connected justice to love. He had optimism about America despite the obvious struggles and difficulties that could easily lead him to pessimism—a pessimism to which he was, at times and understandably, tempted to accede.

King was also a realist. Racism was real, oppression was real, and it demanded a response. Love was not enough without justice, and its pursuits demanded that Blacks have the courage to stand for their rights. He saw the plight for justice as righteous and based both in his theology and in his adherence to the principles of justice in the Constitution: "We are not wrong in what we are doing. If we are wrong, then the Supreme Court of this nation is wrong. If we are wrong, the Constitution of the United States is wrong. If we are wrong, God almighty is wrong. If we are wrong, Jesus of Nazareth was merely a utopian dreamer and never came down to earth. If we are wrong, justice is a lie."[6]

King saw the need to make a case for the reality of structural injustice that necessitated a response that need not be violent but could be violent. In effect, the Black Power movement responded to the same structural reality with a conditional response that saw in the use of force the only effective response to injustice.

In the conjunctive, there is an assertion about a situation that demands a justification. It is reasonable that a state of pervasive injustice will trigger a violent response if those suffering injustices cannot find a remedy—as we asserted to be the case concerning the conditional. The conjunctive is not *proposing* violence as the solution nor establishing that peaceful protest cannot be an instrumental cause for

---

[6] Cited in James H. Cone, *Martin & Malcolm & America: A Dream or a nightmare* (New York: Orbis, 1991), 62.

justice and in turn peace. It warns about that possibility, however, because one cannot exist without the other.

Moreover, justice is not the only social good that brings about peace. As Pope John Paul II reminded us, "No one should be deceived into thinking that the simple absence of war, as desirable as it is, is equivalent to lasting peace. There is no true peace without fairness, truth, justice and solidarity."[7] Special attention ought to be granted to truth. In effect, there can be a claim to justify force built on a false assertion about the presence of injustice.

The determinant question ought to be clear by now: Do the present circumstances merit the conclusion that we live in a systemically racist society that triggers the violence we are now observing? Again, injustice merits a response that need not be violent and the life and efforts of Martin Luther King and his movement show it. King made a case for the presence of injustice and made a case for a courageous but nonviolent response.

CIVIL RIGHTS AND VIOLENCE

The civil rights movement grew out of a profound spiritual conviction that the men and women of that generation were called to ignite the fire of righteousness and truth. It seemed as if God had planned for a people of destiny and Dr. Martin Luther King Jr. was born in the midst of that calling. He was born in an era of social and legal injustice against Blacks, and experienced it early. One day, as a child, he observed his father sit down in the front waiting seats reserved for Whites. The shoe store clerk blurted, "If you will move to the back, I'll be glad to help you." Daddy King refused, the clerk refused to serve him, and Mr. King took little Martin out mumbling, "I don't care how long I have to live with this thing, I'll never accept it. I'll fight it till I die. Nobody can make a slave out of you if you don't think like a slave."[8]

Daily reminders of his degraded state seemed to contradict what he was learning from his dad about human dignity. Why were Blacks

---

[7] Pope John Paul II, Message for the World Day of Peace, January 1, 2000, https://www.vatican.va/content/john-paul-ii/en/messages/peace/documents/hf_jp-ii_mes_08121999_xxxiii-world-day-for-peace.html.

[8] Martin Luther King Jr., *Stride Toward Freedom* (New York: Harper & Row, 1958), 19.

required to address Whites, even children, as "Mr." or "Mrs." but all Blacks were always called by their first names, even if they were elderly? The pain of insulting treatment was worse than what any law could inflict.

The church was the place where he could find affirmation, a second home for a spirit bewildered by acts of injustice that did not make sense. At Ebenezer Baptist Church he could be somebody among a community that affirmed him and saw Blacks as having a high destiny that could not be taken away no matter what Whites did. It was a haven where, even if only for a few hours, Martin could have a respite from those who hated him. That spirituality was planted in him and remained there for his whole life.

There was also an endeavor that inspired him: education. Words engulfed him in a world of possibilities. "You just wait and see, I'm going to get me some big words," he once told his parents.[9] Education also served as a cleansing agent that exorcised the anger and resentment that built up when he was mistreated. In college, he had the opportunity to work alongside Whites who were fighting against racism, people of goodwill. "I was ready to resent the whole White race, but as I got to see more Whites, my resentment softened and a spirit of cooperation took its place."[10] At the same time, White stereotypes presenting Blacks as degraded and unintelligent motivated him to excel, to show them they were wrong. Even when the possibilities seemed grim and the rules tilted to ensure his failure, he succeeded.

Although King embraced Protestant liberal theology, he was also influenced by natural law thinkers of traditional philosophy and the personalist school. He was not far away from Aquinas and Niebuhr. It is as if he was shaping a worldview, an interpretive lens tinted with all sorts of influences that eventually led to an integrationist approach where hope, informed by reason, led the way. Supported by the songs and the faith of Negro spirituality, he began to see the transcendent light that left color behind and affirmed with Paul that we are all "one in Christ Jesus" (Gal. 3:28). The Black church also had a tradition of great respect for the pastor as a caudillo of destiny. King's leader-

---

[9] James H. Cone, *Martin & Malcolm & America: A Dream or a Nightmare* (New York: Orbis, 1992), 26.

[10] Stephen B. Oates, *Let the Trumpet Sound: The Life of Martin Luther King, Jr.* (New York: Mentor, 1985), 17.

ship was honed and his calling for a mission was formed. His studies finished, he returned to a different scenario than the intermittently welcoming one in college; he went back to Montgomery, the "cradle of the Confederacy." By the time that Rosa Parks had enough, King was ready.

This destiny was joined by many others whose incubator was the Black church and whose aim was also hope. They were able to see beyond the degradations of everyday life, embrace a set of truths about the human person, and recognize them in the founding values of the nation. A cry began to build, a cry for justice. "Be true to what you say on paper!" They indeed embraced that meaning of the papyri better than anyone else in the nation. Even as White clergy remained unmoved, there were these prickly truths that mobilized and eventually transformed the nation. There was a price to pay for rocking the boat. King's universalism did not fade even as most of those who preached it cowered under pressure. The Black church embraced the movement, and the name of King's organization reflected its religious roots: Southern Christian Leadership Conference. Its mission was "to redeem the soul of America."

It was that redemptive essence that informed the movement as it challenged America and engaged in an arduous and unprecedented effort, one that called Blacks to pick up a cross. But that cross changed America. It became a movement based on a universal faith in humanity, a courageous insistence on nonviolence even when it seemed ineffective, and an embrace of the values of the founding as these for the most part reflected the natural law of God. It was integrationist, personalist, and hopeful.

We can ascertain that the slogan "No Justice, No Peace" is not useful without a context and without a justification for the use of violence. Those who use the slogan are at times part of the universe at hand and incapable of seeing that it is possible that their violent response might not be justified. They are involved in a "Game Without End," where they can run through all possible internal examinations without effecting real change in their consciousness. Only with a radical leap from the paradigm that justifies violence can we see that their response is unnecessary and that the system they deem irreformable can generate from within itself the conditions for its own second-order change.[11] As slogans are synecdoche, they are created for action, not for reflection. They are shouted, not proposed. They are there to mobilize or delude, separating believers from the hoi polloi. Beware of all slogans.

---

[11] See Paul Watzlawick et al., *Change: Principles of Problem Formulation and Problem Resolution* (New York: W. W. Norton & Company, 1974), 21–25.

6

Is Black Lives Matter the Solution?*

Ismael Hernandez

In recent years, the Black Lives Matter (BLM) movement has come to the forefront of the racial justice debate. Does BLM represent a valid continuation of the classic civil rights movement? Is it the solution to America's race problem? To answer these questions requires analysis of the various elements subsumed in the phrase "Black Lives Matter": the proposition, the organization, and the movement.

The Proposition

It is difficult to find anything objectionable with the proposition. It ought to be obvious that the lives of Blacks matter because Blacks are human beings made in the image and likeness of God. They matter because they are human, as are the members of every other human racial group. In effect, race itself is a social construct that uses certain

---

* Portions of this chapter were previously published as "'One Front of Many': The Marxist Agenda of Black Lives Matter," at https://1776unites.com/essays/one-front-of-many-the-marxist-agenda-of-Black-lives-matter/, and "Black Lives Matter: The Proposition, the Organization, and the Movement," *Religion & Liberty* 30, no. 3 (September 17, 2020), https://www.acton.org/religion-liberty/volume-30-number-3/Black-lives-matter-proposition-organiza tion-and -movement.

biological differences but cannot create a break in nature. Humans remain humans regardless of these divisions created in the course of history. Blacks are among the sons and daughters of God, with an ineradicable intrinsic dignity. The intrinsic dignity of Blacks is a truth based on the general idea of human worth, and emphasizing a subset of humanity might simply assist us in addressing practical realities that need attention. If you are drowning, I am coming to rescue *you,* not the entire human race.

Moreover, to recognize such distinctions is not in itself objectionable. To focus on a subset of humanity for emphasis is normative in the way we analyze situations in context. A good example is when we say that the unborn matter. That statement is not exclusivist, as if it implies that people who have already been born are not important. I question those who strongly object to the proposition that Black lives matter, as this might convey a deficient anthropology that includes racial antagonism. There is no need to react to things simply because they offer an emphasis on Blacks or any other group of people. At times, that might be necessary.

Still, we might ask if an otherwise unobjectionable proposition such as "Black Lives Matter" can be misused. While the phrase does not in itself imply an exclusivist claim, it is possible that it could be intended in such a way: that one means to say that *only* Blacks matter.[1] One can also attempt to prevent others from focusing on other subgroups by demanding that everyone focus only on one's own agenda. For example, attacking those who say "Blue Lives Matter" as more police officers are killed in the line of duty or are attacked as a group, would seem to imply opposition to highlighting the problems of a different group. In a pluralistic society informed by civility and liberty, there will be multiple areas of concern and differences of approach in tackling issues. When a group wants to fill all of the air in the public square, we

---

[1] In its statement of beliefs, the Black Lives Matter main organization—it is after all a network, not just one group—says: "We are unapologetically Black in our positioning. In affirming that Black Lives Matter, we need not qualify our position. To love and desire freedom and justice for ourselves is a prerequisite for wanting the same for others." In other words, they do not claim that only Blacks have dignity but that affirming Black dignity is a prerequisite for affirming the dignity of others. See https://www.Blacklivesmatter.com/what-we-believe/.

must be careful about the agenda that might lie behind the attempt. In short, the proposition can potentially be misused, but its explicit meaning is not only unobjectionable but true—Black Lives Matter.

THE ORGANIZATION

When we look at the organization, however, things get more complicated. We move from the examination of a proposition as it is to the ideological context given to it by the group.[2] Historically, the proposition was created as a slogan within a very specific ideological context, which we know to be Marxism-Leninism.[3] The origin expressed this basic ideological framework through its focus on race, gender, and economic issues as understood by radical progressive politics. It was not human dignity, the natural law, special Christian revelation, Christian anthropology, or basic historic understandings of justice that gave rise to the slogan. It was the plight of Blacks filtered through the prism of a detrimental secular ideology that motivated the creation of a social media campaign after certain racial incidents.

The movement gave rise to an organization from within a radical ideological understanding of oppression. In the hands of that group, the proposition, now a slogan, became instrumental to their ideological goals and a way of framing the question of Black life in America: Blacks are the perennial victims of America. Black life is enclosed within the construct of systemic racism, which is in essence a revolutionary system of thought, not a reformist one. The theory refers to the systemic nature of the society, not necessarily to the systematic or formal steps taken in a process. Blacks are said to be victims of a system that is fundamentally racist and that results in discrimination against

---

[2] On its website, the main BLM group states its ideological foundation: "Black Lives Matter is an ideological and political intervention in a world where Black lives are systematically and intentionally targeted for demise. It is an affirmation of Black folks' humanity, our contributions to this society, and our resilience in the face of deadly oppression." See https://Blacklivesmatter.com/herstory/.

[3] In a now well-known interview, BLM co-founder Patrisse Cullors admits the Marxist nature of the organization. See "BLM Co-Founder Patrisse Cullors 'We are Marxists, we [*sic*] are Ideological,'" June 19, 2020, https://www.youtube.com/watch?v=Pyhy4IvkENg.

minorities even if none of its policies or institutions are explicitly racist. Blacks are said to be victims of an institutional arrangement whose inherent purpose is to perpetuate White supremacy and Black exclusion. Aiming at eliminating overt systematic discriminatory practices, in this view, does not make a dent in a system that is by definition racist. There is no compromise with that system, even if, for tactical reasons, reform might serve a momentary purpose.

If one is not in alignment with that ideological understanding of Black life in America and with the goals necessarily resulting from such understanding, it is reasonable to ask what the organization is doing with an otherwise fine proposition. After all, as stated, propositions converted into slogans can be misused, especially as they can reflect deeper ideological suppositions. A proposition can be correct but become instrumentally negative as a weapon for an ideology. The BLM movement has taken over the consciousness of many in America and it has rendered any rejection as opposing the very essence of rightness and compassion and the just quest for racial reconciliation. When a movement is conceived in such fashion, we must pause and examine its premises, antecedent influences, and philosophical foundations. After all, we might be gravitating toward a movement that is not what it appears to be.

How to know? The founders of the movement are open about the origins, history, mission, vision, and goals of the Black Lives Matter organization. One is not injuring justice and defaming the group when one takes their assertions as accurate representations of their views. In doing so, we can offer an objective assessment of the organization, and those of us who reject Marxism and Leninism can confidently assess and reject the organization.

"One Front of Many": The Marxist Agenda of Black Lives Matter

"Black Lives Matter is intended to be a tactic to help rebuild the Black liberation movement.... It is not possible for a world where Black lives matter if it is under capitalism. And it is not possible to abolish capitalism without a struggle against national oppression and gender oppression. So, the fight against police terror [and] state violence is but one front of many."[4] These words of Alicia Garza, co-founder of Black Lives Matter (BLM), squarely position that organization within a neo-Marxist framework, where a variety of axes of oppression give way to a multifront struggle.[5]

When Karl Marx died in 1883, Marxism entered a crisis. As several of Marx's predictions for revolution failed, revisionists began to offer alternative explanations. Probably the first major revisionist was Eduard Bernstein, with his social democracy construct.[6] But it was Lenin who saved Marxism, not by his intellectual power but by his

---

[4] *Left Forum 2015: Alicia Garza.* Deep Dish (July 6, 2015), https://www.you tube.com/watch?v=JqaHQ3alJlk.

[5] Neo-Marxism has many tentacles. There are modern, postmodern, existentialist, Leninist, Gramscian, libertarian, feminist, and other types of schools of thought within the neo-Marxist universe.

The concept of "front" is a Leninist one. To counter the higher stage of capitalism, that is, imperialism, communists needed new tactics. As capitalist exploitation widens, its victims are not only the proletariat but even sectors of the bourgeoisie and other classes. In his *Two Tactics* Lenin develops the concept of alliances with other classes without merging with them, as a tactic for bringing the various nonrevolutionary victims of imperialism within the sphere of influence of the revolution. That is accomplished through various struggles that are not directly revolutionary but wound the capitalist system. Lenin created a united front of workers, peasants, and soldiers to defeat the Tsarist regime, deeming these collaborators "fellow travelers." By recognizing that the "crisis of Marxism" necessitated the recognition of various intermediate stages before revolution, he offered communists throughout the world a useful tactic to fulfill their revolutionary goals. See Joseph Shoonara, "The United Front," *International Socialism: A Quarterly Review of Socialist Theory,* no. 117 (December 18, 2007), https://isj.org.uk/the-united-front/.

[6] In his 1899 book *The Prerequisites for Socialism and the Tasks of Social Democracy,* Bernstein criticized Marxist theories, especially dialectical materialism, and the absolute necessity of war to accomplish the goals of communist revolution. In *The Communist Manifesto,* Marx and Engels predicted the concentration of wealth in a few hands within the bourgeoisie and the accelerated impoverishment of the working class, which would expedite the final conflagration giving way to communism. It did not happen. Bernstein interpreted Marx's analyses differently and pointed to the stability and adaptability of capitalism. He called for reformist politics in which society and the political and economic system would be changed gradually in an evolutionary rather than revolutionary way.

clever use of tactic and terror to take power in Russia. In the face of Lenin's savage and dictatorial rule, many other communist thinkers in Western Europe began to develop a diverse array of revisionist alternatives, a process that remains underway to this day.[7] An important revisionist effort began in Germany, through the Frankfurt school of critical theory, and it is within that school of thought that we can find a remote precursor to BLM's ideology. *Critical theory* refers to several generations of German social theorists and philosophers in the Western European Marxist tradition, who undertook revisionist studies in Marxist thought with an emphasis on culture—similar to the ideas of the Italian communist Antonio Gramsci.[8] Gramsci understood that the increasingly better living conditions of the working class under capitalism made it unlikely for revolution to come about as predicted by Marx. It was instead through the incremental takeover of the cultural institutions—education, the arts, entertainment, and news media—that revolution had an opportunity to succeed. Subversion was to ignite by coopting the system, not by overthrowing it. This is a significant departure from classical dialectical materialism: culture was more important than politics or economics—thus the popular term *cultural Marxism.*

Their quest was "emancipation from slavery" and the creation of a world "which satisfies the needs and powers" of human beings by transforming *all* the circumstances that enslave them. Many "critical theories" and social movements have emerged that identify varied dimensions of domination and oppression in modern societies, among them "Black liberation" theories such as critical legal studies (CLS) and critical race theory (CRT).[9] Intersectionality and other radical

---

[7] Thinkers such as Herbert Marcuse and Rosa Luxemburg critiqued the authoritarian implications of Lenin's concept of the "vanguard of the proletariat." The fact that the Russian revolution was not brought about in a society with a strong and large proletarian class was yet another element that put to the test Marx's predictions.

[8] An excellent book on Gramsci is Antonio Santucci, *Antonio Gramsci* (New York: Monthly Review Press, 2010).

[9] See James Bohman, "Critical Theory," *The Stanford Encyclopedia of Philosophy* (Spring 2021 Edition), ed. Edward N. Zalta, https://plato.stanford.edu/archives/spr2021/entries/critical-theory/.

twentieth-century theories can also be seen as the late offspring of the aforementioned crisis of Marxism.

Within that general neo-Marxist understanding of oppression we find a concept that has come to be known as *intersectionality*.[10] The concept is an analytical framework that proposes that each person possesses different identities that combine to create a variety of operations or modes of either oppression or victimization. A given person might exhibit different modes such as race, ethnicity, gender, sex, race, class, religion, and disability. Every aspect constitutive of a person, and as an extension, social relations, is a relationship of oppression. All these identities overlap and express themselves as advantageous or disadvantageous, bringing forth relationships of oppression or freedom. There are victims and victimizers, oppressors and oppressed, "us" and "them." These relationships lie at the heart of identity and at the center of politics, culture, law, and all human relations. Antagonism is the very essence of social advancement.

This idea developed during the latter part of the twentieth century in the thought of radical feminist scholars and activists. These scholars and activists referred to interlocking systems or axes of oppression intent on marginalizing people based on certain group identities. *Intersectionality* is a term that attempts to explain these dynamics.[11] Originating within the CRT framework, intersectionality challenged the notion that gender was the exclusive mode of oppression for women. Author bell hooks tells us that intersectionality "challenged the notion that 'gender' was the primary factor determining a woman's fate."[12] A number of scholars working within CRT assumptions

---

[10] The ultimate neo-Marxist influence on intersectionality comes via the cultural Marxism of Antonio Gramsci and his theory of cultural hegemony. These ideas overlap with another important neo-Marxist movement, the Frankfurt School of Critical Theory. The Frankfurt School is associated with men like Max Horkheimer, Theodor W. Adorno, Erich Fromm, Jürgen Habermas, Axel Honneth, and Herbert Marcuse, and was centered on the Institute for Social Research at the University of Frankfurt in Germany.

[11] Arica L. Coleman, "What's Intersectionality? Let These Scholars Explain the Theory and Its History," *Time*, March 28, 2019, https://time.com/5560575/intersectionality-theory/.

[12] bell hooks, *Feminist Theory: From Margin to Center* (New York: Routledge, 2014 [1984]).

proposed that the oppression experienced by White middle-class women is different from that which confronts Black and poor women. Writing in 1988, Deborah King referred to the concepts of double jeopardy and multiple consciousness in the experience of Black women being women, Black, and poor.[13]

Associated with and popularized by law professor Kimberle Crenshaw, intersectionality has gained traction within the academy and the media, where advocates have bestowed on it an aura of factual knowledge of social reality and conveyed the impression that failing to acknowledge this complex web of privilege and oppression is failing to understand reality.[14] After Crenshaw, a number of other radical feminist scholars delved into the idea of intersectionality, including the sociologist Patricia Hill Collins. In her work on "Black feminist thought," Collins explored how "interlocking systems of oppression" affect Black women. Collins stated that "the experience of oppression by Black women instantiates a distinctive Black feminist consciousness concerning material reality."[15]

The proximate antecedent sources of intersectionality are thus radical feminist thought, postmodernism,[16] critical race theory, critical

---

[13] Deborah K. King, "Multiple Jeopardy, Multiple Consciousness: The Context of a Black Feminist Ideology," in Micheline Malson et al., eds. *Black Women in America: Social Science Perspectives* (Chicago: University of Chicago Press, 1988), 265–95.

[14] Coleman, "What's Intersectionality?"

[15] Patricia Hill Collins, "The Social Construction of Black Feminist Thought," in *Black Women in America*, 297, 299–300.

[16] We first encounter the term *postmodernism* in 1979, with the publication of *The Postmodern Condition* by Jean-François Lyotard, where he defined it as "incredulity toward meta-narratives." Precursors to the philosophical movement, however, are found in Kant's "Copernican Revolution," that is, his assumption that we cannot know things in themselves, and in Hegel, Kierkegaard, Marx, and Nietzsche. Postmodern philosophy questions the importance of power relationships and discourse in the "construction" of world views. Many postmodernists appear to deny that objective reality and moral values exist. See Brian Duignan, "Postmodernism," *Encyclopedia Britannica*, September 4, 2020, https://www.britannica.com/topic/postmodernism-philosophy; and Gary Aynesworth, "Postmodernism," *Stanford Encyclopedia of Philosophy*, September 30, 2005; substantive revision February 5, 2015, https://plato.stanford.edu/archives/spr2015/entries/postmodernism/.

legal studies, and the Frankfurt school of critical theory. The ultimate father is Marx. To identify Karl Marx as the ultimate influence is not to say that all scholars and activists working within the framework of intersectionality are consciously Marxist. It is rather that the framework embraces the assumptions of Marxist dialectics. It is in the realm of political and structural intersectionality that we can clearly see the thought of Marx.[17] Even postmodernists such as Michel Foucault, who are nominally resistant to determinism, seem to have embraced assumptions from the strongly deterministic ideology of Marxism.[18]

It was within the framework of CRT that intersectionality originated to explain the connection between race, gender, and other identities. Crenshaw highlighted the disadvantages experienced by members of various "oppressed groups" in a hierarchy of disadvantages caused by intersecting systems of oppression. Critical theory and its granddaughter CRT are part of the historical quest to avoid the

---

[17] In "Mapping the Margins," Kimberle Crenshaw refers to three different forms of intersectionality: structural, political, and representational. Structural intersectionality refers to how different structures in society create a complex system based on classism, sexism, and racism to oppress women of color, especially as it refers to the rape and abuse of Black women. Political intersectionality highlights how the experiences of women of color differ from those of White women and Black men and how political engagement should reflect the exclusion of women of color from political participation and power. Representational intersectionality vies for the creation of positive imagery of women of color, condemns sexist and racist imagery, and highlights the importance of women of color having representation in media and other communication outlets. Kimberle Crenshaw, "Mapping the Margins: Intersectionality, Identity Politics, and Violence against Women of Color," *Stanford Law Review* 43, no. 6 (July 1991): 1241–99.

[18] In his debate with Noam Chomsky, for example, and referring to the aims of revolution, Foucault stated, "The proletariat doesn't wage war against the ruling class because it considers such a war to be just. The proletariat makes war with the ruling class because … it wants to take power." The normative moral standard of "justice" is rejected, consistent with postmodernism, but class warfare and the pursuit of power are embraced, consistent with Marxism. Quoted in Mark Greif, *The Age of the Crisis of Man: Thought and Fiction in America, 1933–1973* (Princeton: Princeton University Press, 2016), 315. See also Stephen Hicks, *Explaining Postmodernism: Skepticism and Socialism from Rousseau to Foucault* (Scholargy Publishing, 2004, 2011).

epistemological crisis of Marxism provoked by its scientific reductionism and mechanistic prediction of the inevitable, automatic collapse of capitalism. A positivist approach to social change under the guise of Marxism as science seems to erase the role of human subjectivity and culture. If the collapse of capitalism is inevitable, then there is no need for an effort to develop a revolutionary consciousness that cannot fail to emerge.[19]

The concept of intersectionality is an element within a project that rejects the positivist thrust of traditional Marxism and elevates the importance of "praxis" as a real possibility for revolutionary change and a response to alienated social existence. The old Marxist emphasis on "proletarian consciousness" is removed from the center. But how are CRT and intersectionality still Marxist? The simple answer was given already: they are neo-Marxist, not traditionally Marxist—for specimens of the latter are museum pieces these days. Marxism remains valid as a general methodological framework for social transformation and the destruction of capitalism, but its earlier expression must be challenged and reinterpreted.

Cultural Marxism as it was developed within the Frankfurt school attempted to reinterpret Marx, and CRT and intersectionality are part of that general effort of extending Marxism by using it more as a template for understanding dialectical social relations than as a scientific understanding of society with specific and untouchable elements. In creative ways, revisionists present a conception of society that can be said to exist in stark contrast with orthodox Marxism while at the same time embracing its general reading of history. This revisionism affects Marxist social ontology, which saw praxis exclusively in reference to labor and the proletarian class. Intersectionality, for example, sees political action in the social totality to avoid what Marxist theorist Georg Lukács called "reification"—the notion that everything becomes an object or commodity under capitalism and persons are more like things than human beings. That is why organizations such as Black Lives Matter can speak of human dignity while adhering also to gender ideologies that see no *intrinsic* dignity in human beings at all. The great enemy of movements such as BLM is not White supremacy;

---

[19] See Douglas Kellner, ed., *The New Left and the 1960s: Collected Papers of Herbert Marcuse*, vol. 3 (London and New York: Routledge, 2005), xiv.

it is capitalism. The Black Lives Matter organization fits within this framework of a neo-Marxist vision of social processes.

THE MOVEMENT

Movements tend to have a center and a periphery. The center of the BLM movement is without a doubt the organization and its aims. We know this because the organization created the slogan, generated the movement, benefits financially from it, conducts and channels activities for it, and perpetuates a narrative through it.

On the periphery of this movement, there were many people who joined because they were more concerned with the truth of the proposition that Black people matter because they are human beings who deserve justice than by anything else the organization seemed to stand for. What is problematic is that the proposition was not free-floating. It was not a theoretical examination of anthropological realities or a general affirmation of dignity seeking reform. It was and remains a proposition converted into an instrument at the service of an organization with a specific ideology. With the 2020 death of George Floyd, more and more people entered the movement, and now it has acquired mainstream status. Those masses on the periphery are being influenced by and unwittingly cooperating with the center, which is ideological. The gravitational pull of ideological movements is quite powerful, and everything that challenges the center is eventually absorbed or expelled. Those who openly reject the center are denounced and said to be against the general aim of justice. Once one is within the whirlwind of that hurricane, it is impossible to go outside on a picnic. That is what we call a united front.

We quoted above the assertion of one of BLM's founders that the movement is a front, and it is important to understand why this is the case. What we know as BLM began with rage at what the organization calls "rampant and deliberate violence inflicted on us by the state." Black Lives Matter describes its origins this way: "In 2013, three radical Black organizers—Alicia Garza, Patrisse Cullors, and Opal Tometi—created a Black-centered political will and movement building project called #BlackLivesMatter. It was in response to the acquittal of Trayvon Martin's murderer, George Zimmerman."[20] The proximate reason to begin the campaign was a specific instance of racial violence that highlighted a system they described as imbued with racism. In effect, they affirm that Blacks are the victims of a global effort to extinguish them: "Black Lives Matter is an ideological and political intervention in a world where Black lives are systematically and intentionally targeted for demise."[21]

Many good people join movements out of concern for a cause and are motivated by the desire to "do something." Once a movement starts, however, it is rather difficult to resist its luring enticements, especially when the system becomes a parasite living off real historical wrongs. It camouflages its true colors by looking like another necessary step on the long American journey for racial justice. This camouflage works, despite the founders of the movement telling us what their ideology is, because people want it to be different and hope to isolate the center from its periphery. But the center sucks you in.

This is complicated by what we know of the organization's ideology and the Leninist concept of the united front, as described earlier. History shows that fronts in the countries experiencing "colonialism" or "imperialist oppression" kept on widening to include more and more non-communist sectors. The communists grew whenever they followed correct united front tactics with other movements. They gained mainstream status and acceptance and were looked upon as the most active unifiers of those fighting injustices.[22] The BLM movement has all the elements of a sophisticated united front.

It is important also that we understand the issues at hand and learn of the competing forces within the civil rights movement that gave way to various understandings of Black reality in America: one integrationist, personalist, and reformist; and the other separationist, dialectical, and revolutionary. As a united front, BLM instrumentalizes the race problem for revolution, but not just race. As we learn

---

[20] Black Lives Matter, "About BLM" (retrieved April 22, 2021), https://Blacklivesmatter.com/about/.

[21] Black Lives Matter, "Herstory" (retrieved April 22, 2021), https://Blacklivesmatter.com/herstory/.

[22] See Anil Rajimwale, "Lenin: Theoretician of United Front," *Mainstream* 52, no. 46 (November 8, 2014), https://www.mainstreamweekly.net/article5296.html.

from scholars in intersectionality and the thought of Black feminist communist scholars, there are multiple axes of oppression and there exists a "triple oppression" of classism, racism, and sexism.[23]

Black Lives Matter's emphasis on "gender liberation" fits within this communist and radical feminist concept of intersectional fronts of liberation from capitalist oppression and its various expressions, one being "heterosexual supremacy." On a page (since removed) about what BLM believes, we read that it seeks to "dismantle cisgender privilege and uplift Black trans folk," as well as to "foster a queer-affirming network."[24] It is under the rubric of intersectionality that BLM activists attempt to emphasize gender ideology and queer theory. Those who identify as transsexual or gender-nonconforming

---

[23] The term *triple exploitation* was coined by Communist Party member Louise Thompson Patterson in the 1930s. Later, during internal struggles within the Communist Party USA, a Black party member, Claudia Jones, criticized the party, made up mostly of European and Jewish foreigners, for ignoring the oppression of Blacks. In her view, Black women suffered discrimination within both the feminist and socialist movements but were the most oppressed under capitalism.

[24] See Black Lives Matter: What We Believe, *Archive.Today Webpage Capture* (June 4, 2020), retrieved April 30, 2021, https://archive.is/oARH0#selection -399.0-423.263. In addition, the page says:

> We make space for transgender brothers and sisters to partici-pate and lead.... We are self-reflexive and do the work required to dismantle cisgender privilege and uplift Black trans folk, especially Black trans women who continue to be dispropor-tionately impacted by trans-antagonistic violence.... We disrupt the Western-prescribed nuclear family structure requirement by supporting each other as extended families and "villages" that collectively care for one another, especially our children, to the degree that mothers, parents, and children are comfortable.... We foster a queer-affirming network. When we gather, we do so with the intention of freeing ourselves from the tight grip of heteronormative thinking.

Their present website has substantially altered and shortened the main refer-ence to their gender ideology agenda and now simply states the following: "We affirm the lives of Black queer and trans folks, disabled folks, undocu-mented folks, folks with records, women, and all Black lives along the gender spectrum. Our network centers those who have been marginalized within Black liberation movements." See https://Blacklivesmatter.com/about/.

(Trans/GNC) are given a place as the most oppressed of the victims of White supremacy, with *White supremacy* being the umbrella term for all oppressions under capitalism, whether the question is one of race or not. The Trans/GNC take the place of the *lumpenproletariat*, the lumpen being in Marxist-Leninist theory the lowest stratum of the industrial working class, including thieves, prostitutes, vagrants, and others at the margins of society. This ragged and dangerous class, "social scum" as Marx called it, lacked revolutionary consciousness and often became pawns at the service of the bourgeoise, but also tended to act as the "bribed tools of reactionary intrigue."[25] However, a neo-Marxist theory such as intersectionality must admit the injustices suffered by the lumpen as an axis of oppression and seems to identify the poorest of the poor and the gender nonconforming with the possession of class consciousness and even with the greatest potential for revolutionary consciousness, as they are the most oppressed. The Frankfurt school's influence in this reinterpretation of Marx is clear and comes directly from Herbert Marcuse, who believed that in the United States the proletarian class was the one that "having been bought up by the consumer society, has lost all class consciousness." The hope of revolution resides, he believed, in the intellectuals as leaders and the outcasts as field soldiers of revolution.[26]

To better understand the gender theory element in neo-Marxist theory, let us take a brief look at second wave feminism and queer theory.[27] There are two main characters in the development of radi-

---

[25] See Robert L. Bussard, "The 'Dangerous Class' of Marx and Engels: The Rise of the Idea of the Lumpenproletariat," *History of European Ideas* 8, no. 6 (1987): 683, https://www.tandfonline.com/doi/abs/10.1016/0191-6599%2887%2990164-1.

[26] Mary Winter, "Class Consciousness and the British Working Class," *Marxism Today* 18 (May 1974): 155. Other radicals who saw proletarian consciousness in the lumpen were Frantz Fanon and Black Panther Party leaders Bobby Seale and Huey Newton. See Bobby Seale, *Seize the Time* (New York: Random House, 1970).

[27] Judith Butler's *Gender Trouble* (1990) and Eve Sedgwick's *Epistemology of the Closet* (1991) are central texts in queer theory. However, informal use of the concept began in the 1980s by scholars influenced by the French philosopher Michel Foucault and his views on the socially construed nature of sexual identity. The theory denies that gender and sex have a biological basis

cal feminism that are essential to understanding its anthropological assumptions. The first is the French existentialist philosopher Simone de Beauvoir.[28] Regarded as the intellectual founder of second wave feminism, Beauvoir had a long sexual relationship with Jean Paul Sartre, one they called a "soul partnership," a nonexclusive and intentionally childless union. In her view, the biological difference between men and women was merely a "brute fact," that is, a meaningless curiosity of existence. Following Sartre, she affirmed that existence precedes essence; that is, everything is given or begins to exist without meaning. We cannot derive any meaning or purpose out of brute facts. This view of reality denies the *principle of sufficient reason*, which states that for every entity *X*, if *X* exists, there is a sufficient explanation for why *X* exists. Matter is just there, they avow; it exists, and that is all there is to it. This view also goes against the traditional Aristotelian-Scholastic notions of the natural order, where things have both *sub-*

---

that is useful to differentiate femininity and masculinity. In effect, both sex and gender are socially constructed for the purpose of social control through the creation of hierarchies of group subordination. Women, trans people, and gender nonconforming people are victims of this essentialist oppression in need of deconstruction. Heteronormativity and gender roles are among other hegemonic power structures because they are institutions that privilege heterosexuality and discriminate against those not in positions of power. See Tara Verma, Eli Chapman-Orr, and Antonix Davis, "What Is Queer Theory?" *Subcultures & Sociology*, Grinnell College, https://haenfler.sites.grinnell.edu/subcultural-theory-and-theorists/queer-theory/; and Jonathan N. Katz, "The Invention of Heterosexuality," *Socialist Review* 20 (1990): 7–34.

[28] Her book *The Second Sex* became a catalyst for modern feminism and established her political and intellectual place, although she insisted that her views were elaborations on Sartre's philosophy. Beauvoir was a Marxist who declared herself a feminist in a 1972 interview in *Le Nouvel observateur*, joining others in founding the journal *Questions féministes*. In her book *Ethics of Ambiguity* Beauvoir rejects the idea of God's existence and the concept of humanity as such. *The Second Sex*, her most famous work, is seen as a reconsideration and radicalization of her previous beliefs. See Debra Bergoffen and Megan Burke, "Simone de Beauvoir," *The Stanford Encyclopedia of Philosophy* (Summer 2020), ed. Edward N. Zalta, https://plato.stanford.edu/archives/sum2020/entries/beauvoir/.

stantial form and *immanent teleology.*[29] Different substances have different causal powers and that signifies they exist with intrinsic meaning.[30] As philosopher Ed Feser states, "For something to exhibit teleology is for it to point to or be directed toward some end or outcome. For it to exhibit immanent teleology is for this directedness to be intrinsic to it, rather than imposed from outside."[31] This is absolutely denied by the existentialist school of thought of Foucault, Sartre, and Beauvoir. For them, there is no such thing as an inherent human nature. As Foucault stated in reply to Noam Chomsky's assertion that "humanly valuable" concepts such as justice, love, kindness, and sympathy seem to possess a "real" essence, "These notions of human nature, of justice, of the realization of the essence of human beings, are all notions and concepts which have been formed within our civilization, within our type of knowledge and our form of philosophy, and that as a result form part of our class system."[32]

For the existentialists, the world is a complex arrangement of parts with no inherent tendency toward the ends they serve, and thus without any telos, as meaning must be imposed "from outside," as it were. As there is no intrinsic meaning to anything in the world, the doctrine of ends and final causes is only an imposed meaning and historically it has often been imposed for the purposes of control. Things do not possess a drive toward perfection or fulfillment in their essence;

---

[29] That is, objects have certain intrinsic or built-in features and exhibit inherent tendencies. A "natural" tendency in the scholastic sense means that a thing has inherent affinities or inclinations, which confer a unity in the object. This unity constitutes its substantial form. The reality of substance confers on the object an irreducible causal power, that is, a power that cannot be reduced to its parts.

[30] For a good discussion of causal powers see Eleonore Stump, "Emergence, Causal Powers, and Aristotelianism in Metaphysics," in *Powers and Capacities in Philosophy: The New Aristotelianism*, ed. Ruth Groff and John Greco (London: Routledge, 2013).

[31] See Ed Feser, "From Aristotle to John Searle and Back Again: Formal Causes, Teleology, and Computation in Nature," *Nova et Vetera*, English ed., 14, no. 2 (2016): 462.

[32] Quoted in Peter Wilkin, "Chomsky and Foucault on Human Nature and Politics: An Essential Difference?" *Social Theory and Practice* 25, no. 2 (1999): 177–210, http://www.jstor.org/stable/23559137.

there is no *causa finalis* and there is no *causa formalis*.[33] According to Beauvoir our bodies are impersonal attachments, somewhat external to ourselves, and meaning is derived from the other side of the mind-body Cartesian split, from being a "thinking thing." We are thinking things or, more importantly, we are "freedoms." That is, a voluntarist power exists in us that fills the gap of meaning. This is aligned, again, with Descartes's assertion that the human person is a *res cogitans*, a thinking being. We are "freedoms" that express themselves in embodied projects using that attachment of extended matter we call the body. It is rather difficult to discern what is the "we" in her description, as it seems to be an invisible, immaterial consciousness.[34] It would be accurate to describe Beauvoir's theory as a sort of *moral* or *attributed* dualism where a person and the human animal do not identify and personhood is socially bestowed, achieved by a sort of decree or recognition or attribution.[35]

But that such "we" is a freedom relates to its indeterminate telos or ultimate end. In a sense, as Jacques Maritain stated referring to Descartes, such a view of the person is a type of *angelic epistemology* where the individual intellect becomes self-sufficient.[36] Maritain calls

---

[33] For a discussion on teleology see Heinrich Rommen, *The Natural Law: A Study in Legal and Social History and Philosophy* (1936, repr. Indianapolis: Liberty Fund, 1998), 40–48.

[34] See Timothy Fortin, "Rival Theories of Sexual Difference," lecture, Austin Institute, April 7, 2021, https://www.youtube.com/watch?v=Thk4xdn21Xk.

[35] The attribution view of personhood is indeed radical, as it tells us that no knowledge of meaning can come from biology or science, as things are what we say they are by attributing qualities to them by way of adhering to our choices as informed by our values, whatever these values are. As values differ and are not absolute, we can have an individual who "is" a female and "is not" a female at the same time, depending on who is making the attribution. It is then in the end a matter of power that determines human worth and all other elements of human life, one being sexuality. For an examination of the attribution view see Robert P. George and Christopher Tollefsen, *Embryo: A Defense of Human Life* (New York: Doubleday, 2008), 124–32.

[36] The essence of rationalism consists in making the human reason and its ideological content the measure of what is: truly it is the extreme of madness, for the human reason has no content but what it has received from external objects. That inflation of reason is the sign and cause of a great weakness. Reason defenseless

Descartes the father of the individualist conception of human nature.[37] Beauvoir might be the goddess of modern feminism's individualist conception of human beings and the triumph of their will instead of the intellect. We can move our will into creating a telos from the outside because we are "freedoms." In contrast to Sartre, who saw each of us as an enemy to each other as we fight to actualize our freedom, Beauvoir said that to actualize our freedom we must cooperate and respect each other, something that aligns with conceptions of sexual cooperation in traditional notions of sexual difference. Men and women must recognize, affirm, and embrace their differences, and only by doing so will they be able to create a condition of equality and respect: "[B]y and through their natural differentiation men and women unequivocally affirm their brotherhood."[38]

For Beauvoir, the goal in life is to maximize our freedom. Now, the history of humanity as it relates to sex is that although sex is just a brute fact without meaning, one sex oppresses the other—the male systematically oppresses the female. Beauvoir then concludes that women are not born women but become women as they take the brute fact of sex bereft of meaning and give meaning to it, instead of allowing men to give meaning to women.[39] The process of reclaiming identity by giving meaning to themselves is what is called *gender*. Thus, sex is unimportant as it has no meaning; gender is what gives meaning to sex. But, again, who has historically defined that meaning? Men have, as they oppress women, depriving them of the pursuit of freedom. Women must transcend, in the existentialist understanding, and, in the words of feminist Sandra Gilbert, "deconstruct the patriarchal

---

loses its hold on reality, and after a period of presumption it is reduced to abdication, falling then into the opposite evil, anti-intellectualism, voluntarism, pragmatism, etc.

Jacques Maritain, *Three Reformers: Luther-Decartes-Rousseau* (London: Sheed & Ward, 1928), 40, https://sylvietheolog.files.wordpress.com/2016/02/maritain_three_reformers1.pdf.

[37] Maritain, *Three Reformers*, 54.

[38] Simone de Beauvoir, *The Second Sex*, 1st American ed. (New York: Knopf, 1953), 732.

[39] Simone de Beauvoir, *The Second Sex*, trans. Constance Borde and Sheila Malovany Chevallier (New York: Vintage Books, 2011), 283.

canonical social norms."[40] That is the essence of Beauvoir's famous book, *The Second Sex*.

As the definition of woman is given by men, she cannot live out her freedom and remains tied to the facticity of sex, becoming a breeder, only having meaning in giving birth and staying at home to give birth to "new flesh." There are three elements that impede women from transcending the facticity of sex: Western society, the Western husband, and women's own compliance. Capitalism, as a creation of Western society, with its concept of private property, becomes another instrument of oppressive men who must own the means of production. Who produces children? Women.[41] Thus, men must own women through either brute force or by "mystification,"[42] that is, by inventing the idea that the nature of women is to become mothers. Motherhood and marriage, in this scenario, are oppressive capitalist institutions used by men as a ploy to define women by the meaningless fact of sex and deprive them of the freedoms they ought to possess. This is the essence of second wave feminism: to eradicate meaning from the fact of sex and demystify women to become the freedoms they are called to become. There is no doubt that Beauvoir states certain things that are true in history, such as the oppression of women, but she encapsulates these within a false philosophical framework that inevitably leads to more radical approaches. The most important of these is that expressed in the thought of Judith Butler and "queer" feminism.

Butler takes the assumptions of Beauvoir and moves them forward while rejecting what in her view was an important mistake in Beauvoir's thought. The mistake is anthropological. Butler denies Cartesian assumptions and thinks that the facticity of sex must be denied altogether. Accepting biological sex as a brute fact grants to

---

[40] See Sandra M. Gilbert, "What Do Feminist Critics Want? A Postcard from the Volcano," in *The New Feminist Criticism: Essays on Women, Literature, and Theory*, ed. Elaine Showalter (New York: Pantheon Book, 1985), 29–45.

[41] See Fortin, *Rival Theories*.

[42] From Karl Marx to György Lukács, Antonio Gramsci, the Frankfurt school, to Michel Foucault and Beauvoir, there is a long history of variants in the use of the idea of mystification. In general, it refers to the masking or covering up of central aspects of society or of social relationships that enable forms of domination based on social and cultural institutions.

sex a prediscursive existence; that is, sex is not a social construct but an ultimate and independent foundational reality built in nature. But for Butler everything that exists is culturally or socially formed. Nothing escapes what she calls the "heteronormative matrix." Nothing escapes the social construction of reality, nothing effaces social laws, including biological self. Here we find the justification for the popular idea of "assigning sex at birth." All identities are socially constructed, and the idea of a given biology as essential reality is an illusion. Science itself is an illusion, as it gives meaning and purports to objectively discern what is nothing.

Black Lives Matter has embraced a queer theory ideology whose anthropology answers the question of what we are as humans in a way that is radically different from the answer given by those of us who believe that we are beings with intrinsic meaning. Their calls for liberation and justice, often given with familiar language, cannot be reconciled with traditional Christian anthropology. The false anthropology of BLM informs their worldview, and that is why it ought to be rejected.

In their view, we are something other than embodied unified wholes, complete human organisms whose very existence entails meaning and purpose. A sound anthropology understands that creation as such is imbued with meaning and God made human beings in his image and likeness, with the intrinsic and existential moral capacity for self-realization. He pronounced us "very good."[43] We were created with the capacities of reason and volition and for each other, for mutual self-giving, for love. Aristotle's fundamental ontology states that all things have "forms," that is, natures or essences.[44] The entire assortment of things in existence also have matter, and

---

[43] "And God saw everything that he had made, and behold, it was very good. And there was evening and there was morning, a sixth day" (Gen. 1:31 RSV).

[44] The great Thomas Aquinas developed Aristotelian principles within a Christian framework. Aquinas sought a harmony between the philosophy of Aristotle and Christian theology, creating a system among the most influential in history. For two accessible books on Thomas Aquinas and Thomistic thought, see Ed Feser, *Aquinas: A Beginner's Guide* (London: One World, 2009); and Brian Davies, *The Thought of Aquinas* (Oxford: Clarendon Books, 1993).

united with form, constitute all the particular things we see around us. The form of things makes them intelligible, and we look at it to answer what things are. Things around us are real, as common sense and experience seem to indicate.

What is most important here is that human beings are not mere reducible substrata; human beings are *primary substances* whose reality is not reducible to their parts—primary sources such as you and me are not reducible to their organs, which are in turn reducible to atoms and so forth.[45] These are individual things to which we can ascribe certain individual characteristics but also characteristics that are shared by the same kind of things that share a *substantial form*.[46] For example, I am an individual but also a member of a kind called "man."

A woman possesses a substantial form. She is an orderly and unified whole with various systems such as a digestive system, a cardiac system, a nervous system, and a specific reproductive system. These systems need very specific organs, such as a stomach, a heart, a brain, but also fallopian tubes, ovaries, a uterus, and so on. The substantial form of a woman is the unified and orderly whole with all its systems, organs, and parts; it is what it takes to be what a woman is. The substantial form is also the source of the unity and function of the parts as a whole, the very being of the woman through the various stages of the life of that woman. The form of the whole of a woman is what accounts for the parts, and not the other way around. The woman *really exists*, and she is not merely a physical thing, or biological forces, or particles devoid of meaning. The woman is not an accidental thing, and all the different things of living experience are really real, not merely accidentally present. These parts are not primary substances. You and I and Judith Butler are real, and science investigates us as real things and aligns well with our experience and intuition. Particles are not the ones writing

---

[45] For a good counter to reductionism see Ed Feser, *Aristotle's Revenge: The Metaphysical Foundations of Physical and Biological Science* (Neunkirchen-Seelscheid: Ediciones Scholasticae, 2019), 332–34.

[46] This is what makes a rabbit a rabbit or a woman a woman. It is the principle of intelligibility of orderly wholes with various systems or parts. For a good summary of Aquinas's principle of individuation see Patrick W. Hughes, "Aquinas' Principle of Individuation," *Episteme* 2 (1991), Digital Commons, Dennison University, https://digitalcommons.denison.edu/episteme/vol2/iss1/7/.

here; *I* am writing here. All the parts in living organisms participate in the life of a whole living being, a primary substantial form.

The irreducibility also excludes the idea that meaning and substance reside in society or in the acting person, who confers significance to raw matter devoid of meaning. This idea of irreducibility makes concepts such as you and me real, but it also makes things such as "humanity" and "universal human rights" possible, as there is a universality built into the nature of things due to their substantial form. The readers of this book came to exist at a point in time when their human organisms came into existence, instead of sometime later when some nonbodily entity made the decision to instantiate their meaning or an individual decided to give them meaning. We are not nonbodily persons who inhabit a nonpersonal body. We are the kind of substance or kind of being whose bodily existence is intrinsic to itself, not merely accidentally so—we have inherent dignity.[47] This is denied by radical feminist ideology and the entire ideological prism through which BLM interprets race, gender, the human person, and society as a whole. As such it ought to be absolutely rejected as a deficient movement.

Taking into consideration these three aspects—proposition, organization, and movement, one who desires to proclaim the truth and do justice but does not want to become a tool of those who cunningly manipulate people must seriously pause before embracing the BLM movement. As the living out of justice does not necessitate a movement, the best attitude is one of healthy skepticism toward the BLM movement and of commitment to getting involved with nonideologically motivated organizations doing positive things in the Black community.

[47] See George and Tollefsen, *Embryo*, 57–61.

7

"Silver Rights"

Finding Future Success
through the Group Economy

John Sibley Butler

The experiment called America has produced hundreds of years of data that allow scholars to model success, to discern what works and what does not work. One of the most interesting discernible patterns is the relationship between modes of adjustments exhibited by various individuals and groups of people and the relative success of future generations. This chapter will examine the impact of models of adjustments and future generations, with examples from groups across races and religious traditions. For Black Americans, scholars have examined the impact of the modern civil rights movement, and there is debate in the public square concerning whether it had a significant impact over the succeeding decades. This chapter will contribute to that discussion by analyzing Black Americans' economic advance, among other variables.

In a market economy, one has to look within the experiences of groups and ask how they utilized markets, or whether or not the entrepreneurial experience was included in their strategy. To put it another way, we have to understand how groups adjust by taking their future to the market (entrepreneurial firms) and how this adjustment impacts future generations. The data are clear that not all members of groups will be entrepreneurial; the question is how will the experience of groups within the same populations differ when entrepreneurship is part of their adjustment strategy. Most Americans took advantage of the "factory" mode of adjustment, which during its heyday produced the best jobs in the Western world. This chapter tackles race, opportunity, and success, and suggests a model that decomposes populations and examines their groups' historic relationship to the market.

It is important to open our minds to think about race in America in a new fashion, which includes putting "White" America to the same theoretical test as other, nonWhite groups. We do not start with what people are, but what they have done. This means questioning ideas in the public square about all people in America. To this end, the first part of the chapter presents an understanding of modeling, with an emphasis on human behavior. The second part presents how the market affects groups of people as they adapt to it, and the third section presents solutions for the future. The final section considers the impact of the civil rights movement on Black Americans.

MODELING AND UNDERSTANDING THE FUTURE

My intellectual understanding of the importance of modeling and prediction came when I was an undergraduate student at Louisiana State University in Baton Rouge. I always had an interest in predicting the outcomes of things, the result of watching my father change the "receipt" for successful crops. My father's degrees were in agriculture, and as an agriculture extension agent his task was to examine soil, rotate soil, and genetically alter plants so that farmers could produce a successful crop for market. I was always interested in modeling people, or looking for the "formula" that made them successful. For parents who want their children to do well, I say, "Show me their friends, and I will show you their future. Don't get married without the promise of financial success." Then they have a model in their head. Indeed, advice for models of the future are everywhere in society. Vernon Parenton, a professor of social theory at Louisiana State University, opened my mind to the idea that human behavior could be modeled and understood under all kinds of circumstances.

Professor Parenton reminded the class that theories in physics can be absolute, with no deviation. Although a variable such as gravity has never been seen, we know that it has an effect. As a matter of fact, once you leave our university and go to the moon, gravity ceases to be import. When one studies humans, variables such as norms and values cannot be seen, but theoretically they have an effect. This is why we pay so much attention to family values, expectations, and institution building. As we think about modeling for the future, we have to look across groups at their value structure and how that structure has had an impact through time and space.

We must also understand that theories try to understand principles that guide the world and stand on their own base. Models are metaphors that try to simplify things and are very comparative; thus we can make a model of a society and say that it is like a machine: if you do this and that, then you will get a certain outcome. Both theories and models are necessary, and will be utilized in this chapter. But we must remember, as Professor Parenten pointed out decades ago, that while rocks cannot change their minds, humans can; thus models for human beings must be used with care. Using models to predict racial outcomes, as measured by a degree of economic and educational success, is thus a daunting task, but they do help to make things clear and interesting.

The theoretical idea of economic adjustment can be utilized to understand how generations "prosper" or do not prosper in America. It says simply that when groups first enter a market economy, those who adjust to the country by starting their own enterprises will have different future results than those who came to America as laborers. This means that the former took their future to the market and depended on their communities to provide the structures for business success. From this strategy came things that we cannot see but have an effect. This includes the development of a value structure, the development of a network structure, and an expectation of success. Historical data also shows that for groups that experience a lot of discrimination from the larger society, this adjustment is imperative for the creation of a decent future for their children. These shop owners—the bourgeoisie or people of means—tend to start a tradition of college education for their children, which becomes a cultural expectation.

The other kind of adjustment revolves around those who enter the country by taking their future to the "factory." Factory work, in contrast to shop owning, was more likely to become intergenerational: the expectation of college and economic advance was not as pronounced. Thus one can account for success for generations across time and space by accounting for adjustment to market economies. This is a model that has stood the test of time in many market economies, and as a model it is something that guides research. The model also allows the researcher to concentrate on what the subject does rather than the race or ethnicity of the group. It should apply to established European groups as well as to more recent newcomers such as East Asians, Africans, and Indians. This chapter examines this model, juxtaposes it to the civil rights movement for Black Americans, and asks what was the impact of that movement on adjustment patterns for Black Americans across time and space.

THE GROUP ECONOMY AND FACTORY ADJUSTMENTS: BLACK AMERICANS

The Group Economy

Throughout history, scholars have documented the relationship among groups of people and how they adjust to market economies. The literature is also clear that excluded groups, or groups that have been discriminated against by the state, create a sense of economic stability by rapidly turning to entrepreneurship, or taking their future to the market, for the building of communities and the education of children. W. E. B. Dubois, in his comprehensive work *Economic Co-operation Among Negro Americans*, specified observations that created the group economy.[1] This section was extensive, and outlined enterprises that were developed by free Black Americans before and after the Civil War. He showed the development of business enterprises, community organizational structures, and housing. He also noted how this was done in the face of severe racial hostility. Dubois notes that "discrimination in certain lines of retail business often lead to colored stores. Clerks sometimes refuse to fit Negroes' shoes, hence enterprises such as the following:

> *The People's Shoe Co.* (Incorporated), Atlanta, Ga. Number of partners or members, about fifty-seven (57): business 1906–1907, approximately $15,000. The charter was granted under the laws of Georgia in in the year 1901 but remained dormant until October 1905, when it was purchased by the present

---

[1] W. E. B. Dubois, *Economic Co-operation Among Negro Americans* (Atlanta: Atlanta University Press, 1907), 179.

owners, who sold enough stock to open the business in March 1906. The officers are elected by the stockholders at a meeting held in October of each year for that purpose and for transacting any other business specialties in the constitution of the corporation. The business has met with the success expected of it by those who we financially interested in it and is gradually increasing.[2]

Dubois noted that as the group economy was developing, enterprises spread like wildfire. Consider the following quotation:

Women's Exchange Frankfort, Ky. Number of partners or members, five (5); business 1906–1907, $1,500; paid up capital, $500. Open March 1, 1906, with $250. We simply desired to awaken interest among our people along business lines for women, as there had been so many failures (men) here. We are all housekeepers. Had we the entire charge we could soon build a fine business; employ one girl. Each member has a day on "duty" to give direct personal attention to work. Unusual, with women, we have never had one unkind word or unpleasant feeling.[3]

Dubois also documented entire communities that were taking their future to the market: for example, against hostility in Mississippi, coming from the Black Codes that limited Blacks in every way. Dubois's work is very specific about Mound Bayou, Mississippi, a community that rose from log cabins to become one of the most significant communities of Black America, or what he called the group economy.[4]

As the years passed, group economies and their effects were documented all over America. The pattern was becoming evident that the results for Black Americans who took their future to the market would be different than those who took their future to the factories. It must be remembered that both are legitimate ways to adjust but the outcomes are different. As legal segregation asserted itself in the South, the Black group economy intensified. Where the most intense racism existed, the Black community was at its best. This pattern of

---

[2] Dubois, *Economic Co-operation*, 169.

[3] Dubois, *Economic Co-operation*, 169.

[4] Dubois, *Economic Co-operation*, 171.

the intensification of racism and the excellence of the group economy can be found throughout the literature since the very inception of the country. As a matter of fact, after slavery Black southerners refined the idea of the group economy as they took their future to the market.

In a major theoretical work titled *Forgotten Citations*, Butler, Greene, and Johnson codified Dubois's group economy by presenting literature that has all but disappeared from the dominant narratives of the Black experience in America.[5] This important research appeared in E. Franklin Frazier's "Durham: Capital of the Black Middle Class," where he updated Booker T. Washington's "Durham, North Carolina: A City of Negro Enterprise";[6] Edward H. Bonnekemper III's "Negro Ownership of Real Property in Hampton and Elizabeth Country, Virginia"; Robert Ernst's "The Free Negro in New York"; Richard C. Wade's "The Negro in Cincinnati 1800–1830"; and Julius B. Wood's 1916 "The Negro in Chicago." *Forgotten Citations* also has sections on all of the institutions that were founded in these cities and represented what Dubois called the group economy.

In the South, after the Civil War, the group economy was augmented by a network of private Black colleges and universities that provided workers for the group economy. All southern towns, both small and large, featured a group economy. Scholarship that delineates this group economy includes Daniel Murray's *The Original Black Elite*,[7] Lawrence Otis Graham's *Our Kind of People: Inside America's Black Upper Class*,[8] Jonathan D. Greenberg's *Staking a Claim: Jake Simmons, Jr. and the Making of an African American Oil Dynasty*,[9] and Margo Jefferson's

---

[5] John Sibley Butler, Patricia Gene Green, and Margaret Johnson, *Forgotten Citations: Black Community and Organization Building* (Austin: University of Texas Press, forthcoming).

[6] Booker T. Washington, "Durham, North Carolina: A City of Negro Enterprise," *Independent*, March 30, 1911, 643; E. Franklin Frazier, "Durham: Capital of the Black Middle Class," in *The New Negro*, ed. Alain Locke (New York: Albert and Charles Boni Company, 1925).

[7] Daniel Murray, *The Original Black Elite* (New York: HarperCollins, 2017).

[8] Lawrence Otis Graham, *Our Kind of People* (New York: HarperCollins, 1999).

[9] Jonathan D. Greenberg, *Staking a Claim: Jake Simmons, Jr. and the Making of an African American Oil Dynasty* (New York: Atheneum, 1990).

Negroland, which is really important because it details the history of Dubois's group economy in a northern city after the Civil War.[10]

The scholarship that details the impact of the group economy, especially its impact on the education of future generations, started with W. E. B. Dubois's 1911 research, *The College Bred Negro.* Dubois showed that the parents of Negro college graduates were professionals or entrepreneurs in their group economies.[11] This research was done nationwide and thus included all colleges in America. In 1946 Charles Johnson followed Dubois's work with the *The Negro College Graduate.* He found the same relationship between family backgrounds and college graduates and added that by the 1940s, Blacks from Dubois's group economy were in their second and third generation of college matriculation. The continued education of future generations of Black Americans who adjusted to hostility through the group economy was delineated in Joseph A. Pierce's *Negro Business and Business Education.*[12] By 1986 Charles C. Thompson could write in *A Black Elite: A Profile of Graduates of UNCF's Colleges,*[13] that students from Dubois's group economy achieved just as much as nonBlacks from "prestigious" colleges and universities.

THE FACTORY ECONOMY

As noted by Joe William Trotter Jr. in "African Americans and the Industrial Revolution," technological advance from Eli Whitney's cotton gin onward had a great effect on all Americans, including Black Americans.[14] But it was the Great Migration after the Civil War that saw over six million Blacks migrate to northern cities. Although Whites' migration also numbered in the millions, scholars tend to

---

[10] Margo Jefferson, *Negroland: A Memoir* (New York: Knopf Doubleday, 2016).

[11] W. E. B. Dubois, *The College Bred Negro* (Atlanta: Atlanta University Press, 1911).

[12] Joseph A. Pierce, *Negro Business and Business Education* (New York: Harper & Brothers, 1947).

[13] Charles C. Thompson, *A Black Elite: A Profile of Graduates of UNCF's Colleges* (New York: Greenwood Press, 1986).

[14] Joe William Trotter Jr., "African Americans and the Industrial Revolution," *OAH Magazine of History* 15, no. 1 (Fall 2000): 19–23.

concentrate on the movement of Blacks. Put differently, millions of people migrated to the North for opportunities—from elsewhere in America and from around Europe and other countries. Milwaukee, Cleveland, Chicago, Pittsburgh, and Detroit led the great opportunity sectors. Indeed, Detroit was then the Silicon Valley of America as the automobile industry ramped up and became the workhouse for some of the best jobs in the Western world. As Stanley Lieberson notes in *A Piece of the Pie*, European immigrants from all over Europe, especially Central and Eastern, did very well when they migrated to the factory economy of the north.[15] They started their migration in the 1880s, along with Black Americans, but the latter faced racial discrimination from many sources, including labor unions. As these northern Black migrants experienced discrimination over the years, they did not develop the same kind of institutional structure as Blacks who depended on Dubois's group economy, an economy that was anchored by Black colleges and universities. Although there were economically vibrant parts of cities such as Chicago's "Black Metropolis," these cities never developed the comprehensive communities, including Black colleges and universities, that were characteristic of, and fed, Dubois's group economy in the legally segregated south.[16] Thus when the blow came to Chicago's Black Metropolis because of the Great Depression, the enterprises in Durham, North Carolina's Black group economy survived.

During the 1970s the threat of international competition went through the section of America that had produced the best jobs in the Western world since the turn of the century. As the automobile industry and other manufacturing jobs declined, the impact on all Americans, including Black Americans, was devastation. The section became known as the "Rust Belt," and individuals who had become dependent on the factory model saw their lives completely change.

In *When Work Disappears: The World of the New Urban Poor*, William Julius Wilson extends his analysis of dysfunctional families and com-

---

[15] Stanley Lieberson, *A Piece of the Pie: Black and White Immigrants Since 1880* (Berkeley: University of California Press, 1981).

[16] St. Clair Drake and Horace R. Cayton, *Black Metropolis: A Study of Negro Life in a Northern City* (Chicago: University of Chicago Press, 1945).

munities in urban cities.[17] In a country hungry for answers to a problem that seemingly will not go away, Wilson's book has stood center stage in the media as an intellectual icon for public discourse. The pathologies and sad stories that emerge from his rich qualitative data and relevant quantitative tables jump from the pages, as bracing as a television documentary.

Although there have been numerous reviews of Wilson's book (and hundreds of other books on poverty that have been done over the last hundred years), all have missed the significant contribution of this work. The strength of Wilson's analysis is the vivid documentation of the experiences and daily lives of people who live in tough situations rather than an addition to our knowledge of why poverty exists. In addition to Wilson's earlier work, *The Declining Significance of Race*,[18] Sidney Willhelm developed the theme of the impact of technology on Blacks and the loss of jobs in a provocative work entitled *Who Needs the Negro?*[19] The hidden contribution of Wilson's work is that it shows us how people should *not* incorporate into American society; that people who follow factories and do not concentrate on the education of children are doomed to have a difficult time as new technologies are introduced and jobs shift and disappear. This is especially true of Black Americans and other groups who have had a tough time taking advantage of opportunities in America. Thus hidden lessons can also be related to the entire American population.

As we seek a productive way forward, we have rich data that allow us to look at the lives of Blacks who chose another way of incorporation into American society than those reported in Wilson's analysis; they chose not to follow the factory model and created an educational group, which enjoys a "promised land" quite different from Wilson's subjects. Indeed, the data are so rich that we can almost create an "experimental design" on the impact of modes of incorporation into American society on Black Americans. When modes of incorporation are wrapped around Wilson's analysis, understanding Black success

[17] William Julius Wilson, *When Work Disappears: The World of the New Urban Poor* (New York: Vintage Books, 1996).

[18] William J. Wilson, *The Declining Significance of Race: Blacks and Changing American Institutions* (Chicago: University of Chicago Press, 1980).

[19] Sidney M. Willhelm, *Who Needs the Negro?* (Cambridge: Schenkman, 1970).

and Black poverty are intertwined into one model that holds vital lessons for the twenty-first century. Such an analysis calls into question, to a considerable degree, the policy recommendations of this distinguished scholar of the social world. It also sheds new light on the civil rights movement of the 1950s and 1960s. In order to tease out the hidden contribution of Wilson's book, we first review its basic findings. We then turn to how his analysis, and future research in this area, can be strengthened. After a section on understanding modes of incorporation, which allows a powerful comparative analysis between ethnic and racial groups, we augment the policy analysis that emerged in *When Work Disappears.*

When Work Disappears: A Summary

Wilson commences his analysis by recreating the history of a poverty neighborhood through the eyes of the people who live there. A once-stable community, with thriving enterprises, busy streets, and safe pedestrians, declined almost geometrically and now is a shadow of its past. It was a community which, at one time, generated its economic life from many factory jobs and other spin-off enterprises which are part of factory towns. Retail stores, restaurants, and service professionals were abundant. This economic structure, which contributed to stable families, excellent role models, and avenues for upward mobility through good jobs, is now a thing of the past. Wilson's more mature respondents recall the days when they could look forward to an excellent work day, a safe community, and the patronage of stores within walking distance of their homes.

Wilson's analysis comes alive through families, and their strategy for snatching a minimum of economic subsistence from the jaws of poverty and devastation—which, of course, is the result of the disappearance of jobs. Familiar patterns of hopelessness emerge in an almost endless stream of paragraphs. Trafficking in drugs is a strong pattern that emerges from his data. We are introduced to a thirty-five-year-old male who sells cocaine because "I have to feed my family." A twenty-eight-year-old welfare mother informs us that when money is short, a person will "turn tricks, sell drugs, anything—and everything. Mind you, everyone is not a stickup man ... but any and everything. Me myself I have sold marijuana, I'm not a drug pusher, but I'm just tryin' to make ends—I'm tryin' to keep bread on the table—I have two babies."[20]

Wilson constantly reminds us that that the urban poor are victims of forces beyond their control that have been shaping American society: the movement of factories from the central cities to the suburbs, the movement of middle-class people to the suburbs, and the inability of the poor to move with jobs. Although this trend has been nationwide, the figures for Wilson's laboratory, Chicago, are powerful. In the beginning of that decade (1990), only one in twelve people in the poor urban areas of that city held jobs. Wilson notes that communities under his observation have been overwhelmingly Black for the last four decades, yet they only lost most of their residents between 1970 and 1990. Thus catchwords such as "segregated" neighborhood are not strong enough to explain the movement of communities from "Institutions to Jobless Ghettoes." Instead, other forces such as the loss of jobs and problems in getting to new jobs are the proper focus for analysis. Put differently, if jobs can reappear, the character and the structure of the neighborhood will also reappear.

Wilson's treatment of "Ghetto Related Behavior and the Structure of Opportunity" is a reminder of how important presentation of self is when individuals seek job opportunities. He provides an insight into a culture that has not been taught, or has been deprived of, the cultural attributes that are important in the world of business. Ghetto-related behavior is defined as behavior and attitudes that are found more frequently in ghetto neighborhoods than in neighborhoods that feature even modest levels of poverty and local employment. Although these behaviors are not necessarily ghetto-specific, they occur more often in ghetto situations. Wilson introduces us to people who do not know how to dress, speak, and present themselves to prospective employees. Isolated from those who understand the importance of self-presentation, these people find it difficult to acquire this important skill that would allow them to operate in the world of work. As Wilson notes, quoting the Urban Poverty and Family Life Study (1987–1988), "'Nonworking poor Black men and women were consistently less likely to participate in local institutions and have mainstream friends [that is, friends who are working, have some college education, and are married] than people in other classes and ethnic

---

[20] Wilson, *When Work Disappears*, 58.

groups."[21] As this analysis unfolds, one is reminded of the writings of Black scholars who discussed the importance of providing social skills to ex-slaves at the dawn of freedom. Throughout the South, schools were set up that taught not only the "three Rs," but also how to talk to customers, tie a tie, and present oneself in public. The descriptions provided by Wilson are a haunting specter of a culture that is neither African nor Afro-American; a tribal culture which cannot trace its roots to an African past or the recent colored/Negro/Black/Afro culture. It is a situation where there is no one to inform people, as in generations past or before other Blacks migrated to the suburbs, that one is a disgrace to the race and should therefore learn the graces of operating in American society.

Coupled with intense isolation is the reality of family problems in Wilson's urban laboratory. He takes us through the traditional issues of birth rates among unmarried women (which has shown a greater increase among Whites than Blacks between 1980 and 1992, the year of his data, a trend that has continued), attitudes toward marriage and the family, single-adult households, the strengths and weaknesses of marriage itself, and the battle of blame between men and women over social conditions. Wilson's situational analysis is strong in explaining these patterns. He notes, for example, that, "In the inner-city ghetto community, not only have the norms in support of husband-wife families and against out-of-wedlock births become weaker as a result of the general trend in society, they have also gradually disintegrated because of worsening economic conditions in the inner city, including the sharp rise in joblessness and declining real incomes."[22]

It is the drama and vividness of Wilson's presentation, rather than the results themselves, that holds the attention of the reader as the contents of the book enter the mind. Like a western movie, the ending is certain; it is only the gory details that hold the attention as the reader is thrown from situation to situation.

There is nothing wrong with adjusting to America through the factory model, as the majority of Americans will do. But the impact of the factory model versus Dubois's group model is significant for future generations. Data from the US Department of Education (1992) are very clear on the influence of the group economy and

---

[21] Wilson, *When Work Disappears*, 65.

[22] Wilson, *When Work Disappears*, 97.

region on the educational efforts of Blacks. In states where Blacks make up the largest percentage of total enrollment in higher education, southern states with the greatest legal segregation laws lead the list. In Mississippi, 27 percent of students enrolled in college are Black. This is followed by Louisiana (24.6%), Georgia (22.6%), South Carolina (21.6%), Alabama (20.1%), Maryland (19%), North Carolina (18.7%), Virginia (14.6%), Tennessee (14.9%) and Arkansas (14.4%). In states where Blacks make up the largest percentage of the total bachelor's degrees awarded in 1991, the list is also southern. They include Mississippi (20.5%), Louisiana (19.3%), North Carolina (14.4%), Alabama (13.6%) and South Carolina (13.4%).[23] It should be pointed out that although historically Black colleges and universities carry a great load of the college graduates, southern traditional White schools have high percentages of Black students. One certainly gets sick and tired of national news stories (usually on communities such as those studied by Wilson) whose theme is that it is a miracle that Blacks go to college. When most American European ethnic groups were being processed through Ellis Island during the late 1800s, over one hundred Black private colleges and universities were already producing college graduates.

THE GROUP ECONOMY AND THE FACTORY ADJUSTMENTS: NONBLACK GROUPS

The same relationship between hostility, the group economy, and success of future generations can be seen among other groups. This research tradition does not recognize the contribution of W. E. B. Dubois and goes under the title enclave theory. But like the group economy theory, it examines how different White ethnic groups adjusted to American society and how they took their future to the market. The first thing to understand is that there is a great deal of variation among European-ethnic groups in America when it comes to the idea of education, which is one important factor in success and an excellent predictor of those who find employment in changing economies. More importantly, where "Whites" find themselves today is directly related to decisions made by past generations. This is no

---

[23] John Sibley Butler, *Entrepreneurship and Self-Help among Black Americans: A Reconsideration of Race and Economics* (New York: SUNY Press, 2007).

new revelation, but as noted above the patterns tend to be related to decisions about working in the factory culture or starting small shops and sending children to college. Alejandro Portes and John Bach put it well as they were trying to understand the importance of small shops and the education of children for the Cuban refugees in Miami; they reached back for a historical comparison in American society and grounded the Cuban experience in the tradition of other groups that had gone before them:

> Two immigrant groups arriving during the 1890–1914 period differed … in the way their labor was utilized in their mode of adaptation.… Both groups were non-Christian, but they were different in religion, language, and race. They disembarked at opposite ends of the continent and never met in sizable numbers at any point. Yet, Jews and Japanese developed similar patterns of economic and social adaptation that were remarkable similar. What both groups had in common was their collective resistance to serving as a mere source of labor power. From the start, their economic conduct was oriented toward two goals: (1) the acquisition of property, and (2) the search for entrepreneurial opportunities that would give them an "edge" in the American Market.[24]

Portes and Bach utilized the importance of modes of incorporation in order for them to understand the rapid movement of Cuban Americans into the economic security column of American society. As noted earlier, modes of incorporation ask us to understand what past generations did when they entered the country. More importantly, the research is finding that values such as the acquisition of property and the search for entrepreneurial activities have a high correlation with the value of the education of children. What is very interesting about this research is that it is groups that experienced discrimination (religious, racial, language) and were excluded from excellent factory jobs early in their arrival that have a tradition of educating their children. This is, to repeat, because they were forced into small shops and other kinds of entrepreneurial behavior.

---

[24] Alejandro Portes and Robert L. Bach, *Cuban and Mexican Immigrants in The United States* (Berkeley: University of California Press, 1985), 38.

The modes of incorporation paradigm is powerful because of its universal application and its effect through time. For example, as early as 1920 European anthropologists were astounded by the emphasis that the Ibo of Africa placed on enterprise, the acquisition of property, and the education of children. The Ibo is an ethnic group that has been persecuted in Africa for hundreds of years, driven from towns and cities, and indeed without an established homeland. But they were always standing shoulders above others on that continent when it came to the educational accomplishments of children. When early European anthropologists attempted to explain the historical success of the Ibo, they looked to their own backyard and labeled the Ibo "the Jews of Africa." The relationship between hostility, enterprise, and the education of children was very clear to them.[25]

As we move across the world, we see the same kind of success patterns today among the hated Koreans of Japan, the Chinese in Vietnam, and the Pakistani in England and America. Of course historical scholarship also noted this pattern. As early as the late 1800s Max Weber, in *The Protestant Ethic and the Spirit of Capitalism*, noted that the pattern existed among the Huguenots (or Protestants) of France under Louis XIV, the Nonconformists and Quakers in England, and Poles in Russia and Eastern Prussia.[26] In *The Jews and Modern Capitalism*, an almost forgotten work that appeared in the 1930s as an answer to Weber, Werner Sombart noted that the pattern had existed among the Jewish group years before the Protestants came upon the scene. The data are quite clear, and there should be no arguments about the relationship between modes of incorporation and the education of future generations.

---

[25] For a discussion see John Sibley Butler, "Why Booker T. Washington Was Right: A Reconsideration of Race and Economics," in *A Different Vision: African American Economic Thought*, ed. Thomas D. Boston (New York: Routledge, 1997).

[26] Max Weber, *The Protestant Ethic and the Spirit of Capitalism* (1905; repr., London: Unwin Hyman, 1930).

Civil Rights Mode
of Adjustments and Black America

The civil rights movement economically benefited Blacks who stood in the tradition of the group economy but did not have a significant economic impact on the poor. As Martin Luther King noted, "I cannot stop them from hating me but I can stop them from lynching me." The greatest impact was the legal protection provided vis-à-vis housing and jobs and the ability to work in local and state government occupations. Coming out of the movement, Black southerners in the group economy tradition had developed a strong history of education and community organizations. Thus, they were the ones who could take advantage of the opening up of the South and their ability to spend their money anywhere. But this also had a big effect on the group economy, although one has to say that national franchises such as McDonald's stifled the effect of small enterprises headed by families. The civil rights movement did not have a strategy to incorporate the assets of Dubois's group economy. Indeed, instead of enhancing the economy, it set out to show how inferior it was so that Blacks could drink at a water fountain.

It should be pointed out that no White or Asian group had to define their group economies as inferior. Enclaves such as Chinatowns and those founded by the Vietnamese still serve the same purpose as the group economy that was developed by Blacks. But there was no civil rights movement necessary to allow other groups to participate in the larger economy. Again, all modes of adjustment are legitimate; they just have different consequences. Thus, among Blacks, Atlanta, New Orleans, Nashville, and Jackson, Mississippi, for example, still have colleges and universities in the Dubois group tradition. Under segregation, homophily (the tendency for religious or ethnic groups to band together to create the future) was very strong. One can imagine what the South Side of Chicago or Detroit would look like today if Blacks there had developed private Black colleges and universities. Compare what happened with White groups such as the Mormons, who received a great deal of hostility, settled in Utah, and developed Brigham Young University.

The group economy and the enclave economy also teach values of entrepreneurship and keep their residents away from non-achieving

Whites who are not grounded in a history of achievement. This theme is explored in Nancy Isenberg's *White Trash: The 400-Year Untold History of Class in America*. This work reinforces that fact that it is not the color of your skin but how you adjust to American society.[27] Her analysis shows how immigrant Whites fought against different theories of inferiority in America. Research has shown that those who took their future to the market, much like the group economy, created a future for their people. Others seem to fall by the wayside, as can be seen in the recent work by Jonathan Metzi, who wondered out loud why poor Whites voted against their health and economic interest.[28]

Data on success in America are rich and how we think about race should pay attention to what people do in the face of hostility. Over one hundred years of data shows us that Black Americans, and others, who took their future to the market produced a better competitive future than those who depended on the large factory society. The civil rights movement produced great changes in removing signs and in securing the right to vote, which are important. But no one came to America to vote: they came to dream big in the largest economy in the world. It has been difficult, but certainly the research shows that where group economies or enclaves are developed, the competitive future is better. This process is being repeated by immigrant Nigerians, Asian Indians, and others as the first generation creates the continuous birth of America.[29] The model for success in America lies in the forgotten citations of Black Americans—and all Americans who understand the relationship between entrepreneurship and success for future generations.

---

[27] Nancy Isenberg, *White Trash: The 400-Year Untold History of Class in America* (New York: Viking, 2016).

[28] Jonathan M. Metzi, *Dying of Whiteness: How the Politics of Racial Resentment Is Killing America's Heartland* (New York: Basic Books, 2019).

[29] John Sibley Butler and George Kozmetsky, *Immigrant and Minority Entrepreneurship: The Economic Rebuilding of American Communities* (New York: Praeger, 2004).

8

THE WAY FORWARD*

Ismael Hernandez

How easily we blame others for our shadows. The boundary between wholeness and alienation runs straight through our hearts, through our consciences, through our beliefs and actions. But the force of a contrary understanding is winning the day. It was Rousseau who started the modern "Age of Alibi," its precursor being Adam, who blamed God: "That woman you gave me ..." Rousseau placed the origin of human corruption in the social order—he was the first to propagate the idea of "structural oppression," later given formal analysis by Marx and recently becoming the central tenet of the racialist ideology.

"We are good; society corrupts us," is the substance of the modern understandings of history and social reality in America. If we fail to achieve the state of nirvana from where we claim to have been unjustly removed, we find an alibi. Evil forces lurking around and planning against us are the culprit. Powers beyond our control prevent our fulfillment.

The task of self-discovery is further complicated when actual historic wrongs have been inflicted on a group. As we can always point out to

---

* A version of this chapter was previously published at the Freedom and Virtue Institute website, https://www.fvinstitute.org/newspress/.

the historic fact of injustice, we can always trace our present difficulties back to that original sin and deny the possibility of meaningful agency. Calling for an alternative explanation where we have meaningful autonomous social space is easily dismissible as an instance of blaming the victim. The perennial question of race and racism today remains parasitic on ignorance of the primary source of our problems: the abandonment of a sound anthropology able to steer us toward sound social understanding.

But, as it remains the case that the matrix of social understanding in the here and now runs through the heart of every life lived, we can easily immerse ourselves in a vicious cycle of victimization, a tendency some scholars have called the utopian syndrome. A utopian is one who sees a solution where there is none and who favors extremism in the pursuit of that solution. When one believes he or she has found the ultimate explanatory element for a condition, the resulting behavior is what we call the utopian syndrome. The counterpart of the utopian syndrome is the *terrible simplicateur,* the one who never sees a problem. There are many simpletons who disregard the question of race as a mere fabrication of leftist ideologues or as a historical datum devoid of present relevance. The problem is that both the utopian and the simpleton disregard anyone who dares to question their paradigms. The easy accusation against those who express skepticism is that of being "ignorant" by complicating the obvious or by disregarding the momentous.

The utopian syndrome has had three main expressions. The first is *self-pity,* where people feel sorry for themselves and invite commiseration—a "poor me and damn them" stance. The second is *nihilism.* A nihilistic life is where immediate gratification is seen as a way to "opt-out" of society into a world of ecstasy and momentary euphoria (sex, drugs, petty crime). The third expression is *rabid activism.* Rabid activism has become the main political expression of the syndrome and has many engaging on a virtuous crusade to destroy the source of the problem, "them." Grabbing the higher ground of the concept of justice, the activist has a "by any means necessary" attitude, where the pursuit of radical changes justifies virtually any action. Radical movements and even terroristic actions can grow out of this expression.

But there is a milder form of this third utopian expression. Most people do not become fervent activists but end up aligning with a vision of the problem shaped by the assumptions of the activist. They do not descend headlong into the world of fervent mobilization but become a vanguard that offers activism an imprimatur. This type of stance is projective, a moral stance of righteous indignation that claims special insight based on the conviction of having found the all-encompassing truth. The adherent of this mild-mannered activism engages the problem of race not as an attempt to analyze it but as a proselytizing and pedagogic crusade. Consequently, those who do not embrace their insights must be benighted, acting on bad faith, currying favors with "them," or the sad sufferers of insoluble ignorance.

The prevailing answer to the question of race is this mild-mannered form of the activist utopian syndrome that has a whole group of people buying into the affirmation that the ultimate explanatory element for the problem of race today is "White supremacy." This element serves to interpret the roots of our founding as a nation, the history of American racism, and the present problems of our people. Any detraction from that fundamental matrix of understanding is a failure to empathize with a struggling people, a failure to understand and a denial of the problem. Any detraction is seen as a form of the aforementioned "simplifier," a simplistic and ignorant explanation serving as a justification to deny the full humanity of nonWhites.

In effect, the premises for the explanation have become more real than reality itself. Reality must conform to the premise, as there is no other way that it could be. Let us hammer the premise in! The 1619 Project is a very influential campaign built on the mild-mannered utopian syndrome, whereby the very existence of our society is presented as having its inception and its continuation in the sin of racial oppression. That sin is said to be ingrained in the very fabric of the nation and can only be extirpated by a renunciation of the values that formed the basis of our republic. That renunciation is presented as a cleansing, when in reality it is based on a radically different conception of social being. It keeps alive the "Age of Alibi," as we remain innocent victims of an Americanism that prevents us from fully embracing our subjectivity as persons with the radical capacity to change our condition through our choices.

There are no real choices as long as we do not discover the truth about the foundations of what supposedly needs to be burnt to the ground. In the end, it makes us victims of forces outside of our control as long as we remain within the sphere of the "White supremacist" ethos. Of course, the revolution will not occur without a reaction—a

111

synthesis cannot emerge without an antithesis. The reactionary *terrible simplificateur* responds, "Get over it! Racism is over. It is only in your head. In fact, Blacks are more racist now."

We are drowning between these two destructive narratives, missing the necessary balance to become effective change agents. I came across this unbalanced approach upon arriving in America[1] and found myself often warned to expect a negative experience, advised to beware of the Whites (yes, "them"). I was told that I belonged to "protected communities," as if our people were an endangered species arranged in a taxonomy. This is why discussions of what "really happened" in a given case involving race are unproductive. In reality, they are not much more than gambles for power. There is nothing to learn from them. We supposedly "already know" that the nature of our society is intrinsically racist, built intentionally for the purpose of perpetuating White dominance. Or, on the flip side, we "already know" that nothing happened, and the media is just arranging things to perpetuate the narrative of racism.

How do we escape this destructive false dualism? In fear and trembling but with courage. We must also see the futility of attempting a solution within the frameworks of false and unrealistic alternatives. I am aware that my proposal is the one considered unrealistic, but false, closed systems reject anything not in their orbit. As we are not utopians, nothing anyone can propose is going to be an easy or comprehensive alternative, only a signal in the right direction for a thorny journey. I am convinced that the great new step of an authentic civil rights movement begins with severing our destiny from the clutches of race-consciousness, where race is seen as central to our very existence.

The rediscovery and embrace of our individuality as persons (notice, as persons, not as islands unto ourselves) is the important first step. The second is a return to an understanding of the civil rights movement as being within the affirmation of the values and principles of the Christian understanding of natural law as embedded in the Declaration of Independence. We must see ourselves as quintessentially American, not as Africans in diaspora.

---

[1] I was born in Puerto Rico, but refer to my move to the continental United States as coming to "America."

ABOUT THE AUTHORS

JOHN SIBLEY BUTLER holds the J. Marion West Chair for Constructive Capitalism in the Graduate School of Business at the University of Texas. He is a professor in the Management Department and holds a joint appointment in organizational behavior in the College of Liberal Arts, where he holds the Darrell K. Royal Regents Professorship in Ethics and American Society (Sociology). He has appeared on over thirty radio and television programs, including *Eye On America* (CBS Nightly News) and *The Jim Lehrer News Hour*, and his research has appeared in the *Wall Street Journal*, the *New York Times*, the *Chicago Tribune, Time Magazine*, and *U.S. News and World Report*. His books include *Entrepreneurship and Self-Help among Black America: A Reconsideration of Race and Economics*; *All That We Can Be: Black Leadership and Racial Integration the Army Way* (with Charles C. Moskos); *Immigrant and Minority Entrepreneurship: The Continuous Rebirth of American Communities* (with George Kozmetsky, forthcoming); and *Forgotten Citations: Studies in Community, Entrepreneurship, and Self-Help among Black-Americans* (with Patricia Gene Greene and Margaret Johnson, forthcoming). He received his undergraduate education from Louisiana State University and his PhD from Northwestern University.

ISMAEL HERNANDEZ is the founder and president of the Freedom & Virtue Institute. He worked in an inner-city ministry in Florida for fifteen years before he founded the Freedom & Virtue Institute in 2009. He regularly lectures for the Acton Institute in Grand Rapids, Michigan, and has lectured for the American Enterprise Institute, the Heritage Foundation, the Foundation for Government Accountability, and the Foundation for Economic Education. His writings have appeared in *Religion & Liberty, Crisis, World,* and the *Washington Times.* He is the author of *Not Tragically Colored: Freedom, Personhood, and the Renewal of Black America.* He holds an MA in political science from the University of Southern Mississippi.

KEVIN SCHMIESING is the director of research at the Freedom & Virtue Institute. His publications include *Merchants and Ministers: A History of Businesspeople and Clergy in America; One and Indivisible: The Relationship between Religious and Economic Freedom* (editor); *The Spirit Matters: Reflections on Economics and Society Twenty-Five Years after the Fall of Communism* (editor); and *Within the Market Strife: American Catholic Economic Thought from* Rerum Novarum *to Vatican II.* He teaches Church history for the Archdiocese of Cincinnati's Lay Ecclesial Ministry Program and appears weekly on EWTN Catholic Radio Network's *Son Rise Morning Show.* He holds a bachelor's degree from Franciscan University of Steubenville and a PhD from the University of Pennsylvania.